AT THE TURNIN
A BOOK ON SOLAR

MW00776920

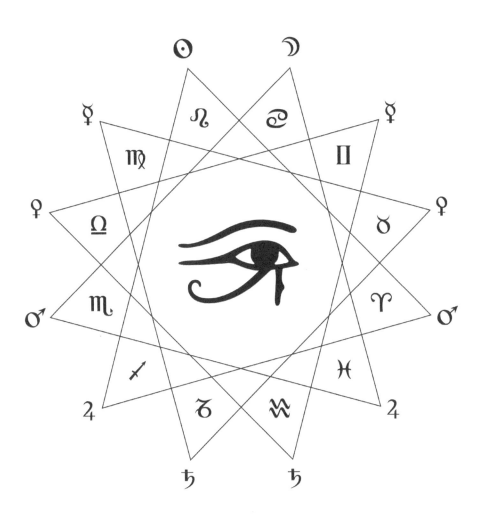

ROK KORITNIK
FOREWORD BY ANTHONY LOUIS

AT THE TURNING OF YEARS
Author: Rok Koritnik
Publisher: Self-published
Year of publication: 2022
First edition

ISBN 978-961-07-1084-4
COBISS.SI-ID 104442371

Copyright © Rok Koritnik 2022

www.rokkoritnikastrologer.com

No part of this publication shall be reproduced or transmitted in any form or by any means without the prior consent or permission from the author.

Cover design: Rok Koritnik

INDEX

INVOCATION   1

FOREWORD   3

WORDS OF GRATITUDE   7

PREFACE   9

CHAPTER 1 – Essential concepts   13

    Sect   13

    Angular strength   15

    Reception   17

    Dodekatemoria   18

    The Lots   21

    Dignity   24

CHAPTER 2 – Annual profections   27

    Definition   27

    Transmissions and the ruler of the year   28

    Setting up a context – the cycle ruler   27

CHAPTER 3 – Solar returns   33

    Significance of Solar returns   33

    Methodology for reading Solar returns 34

CHAPTER 4 – Determining the month   37

    Monthly profections   37

    Timing in Solar returns   38

CHAPTER 5 – Relationships & marriages   41

CHAPTER 6 – Childbirth   71

CHAPTER 7 – Illnesses, accidens & surgeries   99

CHAPTER 8 – Milestones & turning points   131

CHAPTER 9 – Additional time-lords   161

APPENDIX 1 – Example horoscopes data   183

APPENDIX 2 – Notes & bibliography   185

ABOUT ME   187

*May the self-illumined Sun, the light of the world
give us the vision of One in many and Timeless in time.*

FOREWORD

The Blending of East and West

Imagine, if you will, traveling back in time and practicing astrology somewhere along the silk road that connected Asia with the Mediterranean sea. From time to time you meet astrologers from Persia, India, Egypt, Arabia, and you ask them to teach you their methods of forecasting. After a while, you have amassed a huge volume of predictive techniques – some quite intricate and complex, requiring sophisticated mathematics – and others quite simple and straightforward, but almost too simple to be believable. What to do? Being empirically minded (no-nonsense Saturn rules your natal Ascendant and occupies pragmatic Virgo in your birth chart), you decide that the proof of the pudding lies in the eating. You begin to apply the various techniques you learned to the charts of people you know to check how well they work in practice. After a while, a pattern emerges. Highly complex techniques are not always the most effective, and deceptively simple methods sometimes prove to be most reliable. The outcome of your research is a set of predictive techniques which can be applied, using basic arithmetic, to produce accurate results a good part of the time. Your delighted clients tell their friends about your readings, your practice booms, and your reputation as a skilled predictive astrologer spreads throughout the land.

Fast forward a millennium or so, to the year 2022, and you will find that astrologer Rok Koritnik has taken a similar journey. Having learned many of the intricacies of Indian astrology, he also immersed himself in Hellenistic and medieval Arabic and

Persian sources to study the predictive techniques of Western horoscopic astrology. Applying various Western and Indian astrological techniques to charts of his clients, he became aware that the complexity of a method does not necessarily correlate with its accuracy or effectiveness but, instead, can result in an overload of detailed information, which can make it difficult to see the forest for the trees. After much trial and error, he identified the predictive methods that were most consistently reliable and easiest to use, even without a computer. He also established a sequence of steps to follow, to most effectively combine the various techniques. This book presents a straightforward and easily applied method of prediction, which utilizes the blended wisdom and experience of generations of Hellenistic, Arabic, Persian and Indian astrologers. To quote Rok verbatim, "the aim of this book is to present a methodology that is simple, based on whole sign houses and aspects, and which can be easily practiced without a computer." There are also numerous case examples which demonstrate how to use the method and how effective it is in practice.

A core feature of the system is the use of "time-lords" – the idea that the various planets become dominant symbols (lords of time) at certain periods in our lives, so that whatever that planet signifies in your birth chart is likely to manifest at that time. The simplest time-lord system is that of annual "profections" in which the ruler of the natal Ascending sign is time-lord for the 1st year of life, the ruler of the 2nd sign of the birth chart rules the 2nd year of life, and so on around the horoscope wheel, for the rest of one's life. Rok notes that the Nadi astrologers of India use the method of profections, without resorting to other techniques, to accurately predict events. Not surprisingly,

4

profections (both annual and monthly) have become a core feature of Rok's system. He combines profections with another powerful ancient technique – the transits in effect at the moment the Sun returns to its natal position each year – the so-called Solar Return. While trying to keep the system as streamlined as possible, Rok also makes use of other classical ideas such as sect (day versus night charts), dodekatemoria (12th parts), Lots (aka Arabic parts), and the basic meanings of the planets, zodiac signs and 12 Hellenistic "places" of the horoscope. If all of this sounds a bit abstract and theoretical, let me demonstrate with a bare-bones example from my own chart, based on some of the methods described by Rok in his book.

I was born with Libra rising and Aries on the 7th cusp of marriage. My 7th house is unoccupied, and its ruler Mars lies in Gemini in the 9th place of religious ceremonies. Mercury rules the 9th place, disposes 7th-ruler Mars, and occupies Leo in the 11th place of my chart. My marriage took place when I was 32 years old. My annually profected Ascendant at age 32 was Gemini, the sign on the natal 9th cusp and dispositor of natal Mars, which rules the natal 7th of marriage. My solar return at age 32 had Cancer rising, with Mars and Jupiter in Cancer in the 1st Hellenistic place, Moon in Taurus in the 11th place, and both Venus and Saturn in Leo in the 2nd place of the return chart. In the profected chart, Jupiter rules the 7th of marriage; in the return chart, Jupiter occupies the first place, together with Mars, which rules the 7th place of marriage in the birth chart. Rok points out that the 3rd place is also significant for marriage because it is the 9th (religious ceremonies) from the 7th (partnerships). In my profected chart at age 32, Leo rules the 3rd place. In my solar return that year, Venus (love, marriage) and

Saturn (long-term commitment) both occupy Leo. In the solar return, the Moon in Taurus, by monthly profection, arrives at Leo in December of that year. My marriage took place in mid-December. Rok's techniques accurately pinpointed the year and month of my wedding.

Let me conclude by stating how delighted and honored I was when Rok asked me to write a foreword for his book. I have followed his astrological work online for several years and have been consistently impressed by his scholarship, creativity and depth of understanding. In addition, we have had the opportunity to speak personally several times via the internet. Astrologers familiar with the classical Hellenistic, Arabic, Persian and Indian texts will be impressed by how well Rok had culled and blended various effective predictive techniques to produce a reliable and easy-to-use system of forecasting. Those unfamiliar with the classic works may have a bit of a learning curve, but the effort is well worth the payoff in the accuracy of their astrological predictions.

Anthony Louis
March 2022

WORDS OF GRATITUDE

My heart-felt gratitude goes to all the wonderful people who inspired me and helped me in one way or another on my astrological journey or in the process of writing this book. My thanks go to Anthony Louis without whose unselfish help and guidance I would probably never be in a position to write this book, to Aswin Subramanyan, Levi Cosijn, Kevin Lopez and Lars Panaro for their countless astrological conversations with me, to Jean Cremers for developing the wonderful Planet Dance software which made my research work much easier, to Robert Nagy for developing an equally wonderful Traditional Morinus software which I used for the graphical representation of the horoscopes in this book, to Dhyan Dejan Cirkvenčič for his help with design, to Ella Klyashitsky for her proofreading work, to my friends and clients who have allowed me to use their horoscopes as examples, to all the great astrologers of antiquity for providing us with invaluable astrological writings, to all the scholars of Project Hindsight who brought the ancient astrological texts out from the academia to the public, to Chris Brennan for his monumental book which inspired me to dive into Hellenistic astrology, to Anthony of Seven Stars Astrology for the inspiring blog, to my wife and family for giving me the time and support, and I am of course immensely grateful to you, the reader.

PREFACE

Astrology is a complex science and usually it is thought that the more complex, mathematical and scientific one's techniques are, the more their system enables them to predict with a greater accuracy. When I started out to explore this science I quickly followed suit and searched for mathematical precision and complexity only to soon find that while reading a horoscope in such a manner might be a joyful undertaking for some, this surely wasn't the case for me as I felt like I had too much information to read from. It seemed like I was using only the rational mind and neglected the very important element in every system of divination – intuition. This was especially true when it came to forecasting of events. Having multiple time-lord[1] systems at my disposal, one more complex than the other, created unnecessary clutter and obscured my vision. The greatest challenge we face when using time-lords is the lack of a clear methodology and congruity. I have seen that many traditional astrologers, past and present tend to combine time-lords from different time-lord systems, read aspects between them, etc., which always raised a few question marks for me. Because of this incongruity and lack of a clear methodology, I soon felt an urge for a simple but effective predictive system that doesn't overwhelm the astrologer's rational mind and is so orderly that one can picture the whole system with the mind's eye and use it without any aid from computer software.

When I was a beginner astrologer (which in many ways I still am) I thought: "Why not simply move the ascendant one sign forward each year? It makes sense to me to do that." I was surprised to later discover that this technique called profection was the most widely spread predictive technique found in classical astrological texts, from Hellenistic, Perso-Arabic and even Indian tradition. My thought was, that if it was used by most classical astrologers, that there has to be something valid about it, even though it's so incredibly simple. At that time I had been empirically testing many popular timing methods from different traditions. To my great surprise and joy, profections used together with Solar returns have outperformed all of the techniques I've tested (excluding primary directions[2]).

This method of moving the ascendant forward at each birthday goes by different names. In English we call it Profections, in Greek it is called *teleiōsis*, in Latin *profectio*, in Arabic *intihā* and in the Indian Nadi branch of astrology they nowadays call it Bhrigu chakra paddhati (the cyclical method of Bhrigu Rishi), but in the popular Brihat Parashara Hora Shastra it is called *sudarśana cakra daśā*, the word *cakra* (a wheel) pointing to its cyclical nature based on the Zodiac. It was the practice of certain contemporary Nadi astrologers that made me pay more attention to profections, because they predict events by using profections only, without any other timing system whatsoever. The aim of this book is not to demonstrate this almost mythical predictive power, but to present how timing methods that are based on the principle of 1 sign = 1 year, on the 12 year cycle and on the Sun's annual return to the natal position, can be used effectively without resorting to more complex timing methods, which in live readings are often impractical.

I wanted this book to be concise, thus I have omitted any type of astrological basics other than briefly explaining some important principles that are unique to the Hellenistic tradition which forms the basis for this material. It is assumed that you, the reader are well versed in the symbolism of planets, signs, houses and aspects.

In this book I have decided not to use the horoscopes of famous people for a simple reason: I was never asked by any to read their horoscope and I prefer to analyze charts of people who have actually come to me for counseling and have given me their permission to use their charts for teaching.

CHAPTER 1
ESSENTIAL CONCEPTS

1. Sect

Modern Western astrology, as well as modern Indian astrology to a large degree ignore whether the native was born during the day or during the night. In Hellenistic and Perso-Arabic astrology this distinction is of a fundamental importance, and many other concepts and techniques were built upon it. Since the astrology of the Hellenistic tradition forms the basis of this book, we shall now familiarize ourselves with this important principle of sect.

It is natural that we associate the Sun with day and the Moon with night as they are both luminaries that provide light, the Sun during the day and the Moon during the night. They have a status that is different from that of the other five non-luminaries. The Sun is self-illumined, thus representing spirit or consciousness while the Moon being the largest reflector of the Sun's light and being tied to the Earth represents our mind-body complex through which consciousness is experiencing the reality of the Earthly plane. They are God and Goddess, Teo and Tea, king and queen, who have their agents, the other five wandering stars (planets) at their disposal.

DAY	NIGHT	
☉	☽	
♃ ♄	☿	♀ ♂

The Sun who rules the day is joined by Jupiter and Saturn, one benefic and one malefic. The Moon who rules the night is joined by Venus and Mars, again, one benefic and one malefic. Mercury is neutral and can belong to either sect. If it rises before the Sun it is of the diurnal sect and if it rises after the Sun it belongs to the nocturnal sect.

It is reasonable for Jupiter, a hot planet, a benefactor, a counselor, a priest, a sage to be joined with the Sun, the king during the day. But, why would Saturn, the cold planet of darkness, a democrat, a beggar, a street sweeper, a plague bringer join the Sun in the diurnal sect? One answer could be that in the night sect his coldness and darkness would increase which would make him ineffective, thus he prefers to be in the warm day sect where he gets tempered. The other answer could be that the warm and bright diurnal sect must be balanced within itself by a cold, dark force, similar to the Taoist concept of yin and yang, where each of the two polarities also contain a bit of the opposite. It is worth considering that Saturn's hard labor, farming, serving, begging, etc., are activities mostly done in the light of day.

If Saturn seems out of place in the diurnal sect, then Mars seems a bit out of place in the nocturnal sect as well. It is understandable that the gentle, cool Venus, a benefactor, a beautifier, an artist, a love maker prefers to serve the Moon, the queen of the night. But why the hot, sharp, brutal, jealous and cruel Mars, a soldier, a murderer, a thief, a drunkard would want to live in the nocturnal sect? One possible answer is that in the night sect his heat and cruelty get tempered, so he is able to be constructive. Another answer is that the night also needs to be balanced within itself and thus requires a hot malefic. Also, many Martian activities are quite at home in the darkness of the night.

Having looked at the conceptual and philosophical basis for the way sect is assigned, the practical application of this principle is quite straightforward and is a quick and essential way to determine the auspiciousness of a planet. The benefic which is out of sect (Venus by day and Jupiter by night) will be less beneficial as it finds itself in an environment that is not the most suitable. There are of course many shades between total in-auspiciousness and only being slightly hampered. If a diurnal planet is below the horizon in a night chart, then although it is out of sect, it is at least in the bright part of the sky where it belongs[3]. This mitigates its out-of-sect status to an extent. The same can be said if it is placed in a diurnal (masculine) sign. Conversely, if a nocturnal planet is below the horizon in a day chart, then it is at least in the dark part of the sky where it belongs. Similarly, its out-of-sect status is not as pronounced if it is in a nocturnal (feminine) sign[4].

While benefics can still indicate positive outcomes even though being out of sect, it is the malefic Mars and Saturn that can become very problematic when they have this status.

2. Angular strength

Few concepts have been emphasized in classical astrology as much as the angles, or pivots and their importance continues to be recognized in modern astrology to this day. When we asses angular strength we look at the points where planets rise, culminate, set and anti-culminate. These four points are:

1. **Ascendant** – intersection of eastern horizon with the ecliptic
2. **Descendant** – intersection of western horizon with the ecliptic
3. **Medium Coeli (MC)** – intersection of the meridian with the ecliptic above the horizon
4. **Immum Coeli (IC)** – intersection of the meridian with the ecliptic below the horizon

The Ascendant is the most important of the four, because it is at this point that planets rise and become visible. The second in importance is **the MC** where planets reach their highest altitude. Planets that are approaching the four angles are considered busy and loud, ready to act and strongly expressed. When they pass these points their strength diminishes. It is usually thought that when a planet is 15 degrees before the pivotal point it is becoming busy and is at its maximum strength when upon that point. When it crosses over this angular degree it looses its strength faster than it gains it and when it is 5 degrees past this point its strength is already weakened. In the practical examples that follow we will see how angular strength plays a very important role in Solar returns. Please note that it is necessary to look at the exact points and not whole-sign places for this purpose as the MC / IC axis often shifts from the 10th whole-sign place to the 9th or 11th, or at locations far north or far south it can even shift to the 8th or 12th sign from the Ascendant.

Also important is the **Nonagesimal** – the highest point of the ecliptic which is 90 degrees from the Ascendant and is the cusp of the 10th place in the equal house system. Along with the Nonagesimal the whole 10th sign from the Ascendant is also of great importance as it is the place of actions, public visibility, career and authority. The MC mostly falls in the 10th place, but at times it can fall in the 11th or 9th and at more extreme northern or southern latitudes it can even fall in the 8th or 12th place. Even when the MC is in these so-called bad places it still represents the point where the celestial bodies reach their highest altitude if we face due south. In this way the prominence and actions related to the MC get connected with a place other than the 10th.

3. Reception

Reception is an important principle within the aspects doctrine. It can be thought of as an affirmation of the engagement of two planets that are in a whole sign aspect. The idea of reception is very straightforward. It happens when a planet that is not in its domicile or exaltation is aspected by the domicile or exaltation ruler of that sign. That planet is considered to be received, or welcomed in that sign. The aspect of the sign's ruler gives the planet permission to function in that sign and empowers it with the resources. Reception also serves as a mitigating factor. If the planet happens to be debilitated in the sign and the ruler of that sign is aspecting it, then the debilitation can be mitigated, provided the ruler of the sign is in a good condition. An especially powerful form of reception is mutual reception, which occurs when two planets interchange their domiciles or signs of exaltation. In this way they are assisting each other.

4. Dodekatemoria

The Zodiac which we are familiar with is a twelve-fold division of the ecliptic. In classical astrology these thirty degree segments (the zodiacal signs) were further divided into smaller parts. Different sub-divisions were used for different purposes. None of the sub-divisions of the Zodiac comes to mind as naturally and intuitively as the division of one sign into twelve parts. If we were asked to divide one zodiacal sign into smaller segments, it would be perfectly reasonable to create a micro-zodiac within one sign. In Hellenistic tradition this is called *dōdekatēmoria*. The name simply means twelve parts, *dōdeka* meaning twelve and *moria* meaning parts. This division seems to be almost as old as the Zodiac itself and while different traditions use various sub-divisions, the 12th parts are universal and are also found in medieval Perso-Arabic system as well as in most branches of Indian astrology where they are called *dvādaśāṁśa*, again meaning twelve parts - *dvādaśā* meaning twelve and *āṁśa* meaning a part. The use of the 12th parts seems to be better documented in Hellenistic and Perso-Arabic traditions and the same approach to using them will be used in the practical examples in this book. For better readability I will use the term *dodekatemoria* (without diacritics) for plural and *dodekatemorion* for singular, because writing them as 12th parts might be a bit confusing as I'll be writing the places (houses) as 1st to 12th in the same style.

The twelve segments of a sign flow in the natural order of the zodiacal signs, but they always begin with the *dodekatemorion* of the sign itself.

It is quite easy to determine in which *dodekatemorion* a particular planet is by looking at its degree and seeing in which of the 2.5 degrees segment of the sign it is located. However the more precise calculation gives us the exact degree of a planet's *dodekatermorion* placement, which is what is needed if we want to use *dodekatemoria* in the traditional Hellenistic way, that is, placing these secondary planetary positions on inside or the outside of the chart.

The calculation method for calculating the *dodekatemoria* to a degree is as follows:

1. Find the degree and minute of the planet.
2. Multiply the degrees by 12.
3. Multiply the minutes by 12 and convert the result into degrees and add it to degrees from step 2.
4. Add the result to 0 degrees of the sign the planet is in.
5. You arrive at the exact 12th part position.

As an example, let's take the Sun at 15 degrees and 15 minutes of Leo. First, we multiply 15 degrees by 12 which results in 180 degrees. Then we multiply 15 minutes by 12 and we get 180 minutes, which we convert to 3 degrees. Now we have 183 degrees altogether. We add this figure to 0 degrees of Leo, which brings us to 18 degrees of Aquarius, which is the degree of our calculated *dodekatemorion* of the Sun.

Firmicus Maternus, a 4th century astrologer from Sicily stresses the importance of *dodekatemoria* and writes:

> *"Now I shall briefly set forth what you want to know about the dōdekatēmoria. Some people think that from these the whole essence of the chart can be found and they claim that whatever is hidden in the chart can be revealed by the dōdekatēmoria."* (Mathesis, book 2, chapter 8)

By calculating the *dodekatemoria* we get secondary or hidden placements of planets or points. A planet is therefore present at two locations in the Zodiac at once, as if it is present in another sign through its invisible twin and can influence the matters of that place through it's mystical power. The use of the *dodekatemoria* can help us see if two planets that don't see each other and are in aversion are truly disconnected. If the *dodekatemorion* of one planet is conjunct another planet, this certainly connects the two. Another connection is, of course if the *dodekatemoria* of both of them are conjunct. At this point I have to emphasize that **there is only one sign of a particular polarity, modality and element**, thus only one Aries (one cardinal fire), one Taurus (one fixed earth), etc. Thinking that the Aries *dodekatemorion* is something other than the "original" Aries is incorrect. They are both one and the same with the *dodekatemorion* being a fractal, or to express it in simple terms - the same thing on a micro level.

In Hellenistic astrology the *dodekatemoria* were not used to asses dignity, but in Indian astrology its importance was almost on par with the radix placement.

"The influence (of the planets) in the degrees of their exaltations is complete; … in their dvādaśāṃśas, as in their houses;..." (Yavanajataka, chapter 8, verse 1)

The effects described in regard to individual signs apply to dvādaśāṃśas of each sign as well. (Saravali, chapter 51, verse 110)

In the examples in this book I will use both, looking at the alternative placement of a planet by its *dodekatemorion* and looking at the sign of the *dodekatemorion* as a modification of dignity / nature.

In the natal charts of the following chapters the *dodekatemoria* will be drawn on the outside of the wheel chart.

5. The Lots

If I had to pick one of the more subtle elements of astrology to use it would be the Lots. The Lots are mathematical points that are usually calculated by measuring the distance between two planets, or a planet and an angle. This distance is then added to or subtracted from the Ascendant's degree. Planets and places carry significations of concrete manifestations such as Sun as father, Moon as mother, Mars as siblings, Mercury as friends, Venus as lovers, Jupiter as teachers, Saturn as old people, but they signify many more things. Therefore having these mathematical points which carry a much more specific symbolism is crucial. Firmicus Maternus stresses the importance of the Lots:

21

We shall therefore show what you ought to look for in each house and to what extent. For neither does the fourth house from the Ascendant show the parents and the life of the parents, nor the seventh the marriage partner, nor the fifth the children, nor the third the siblings, nor the sixth illness... Therefore, you will always find the House of the Father especially by this method. (Mathesis, book 6, chapter 32)

In this chapter he describes 24 lots and their calculation. In this book we will use some of the Lots mentioned by him, and also some given by Dorotheus of Sidon, Vettius Valens and Paulus of Alexandria. The importance of the Lots became obvious to me during the process of testing and compiling the example material for this book. They provide an invaluable additional testimony without which the astrological picture we are looking at remains hazy, especially so in the Solar return charts. I find that the most important factor to consider is the planet that is ruling the Lot, or if there is an important planet conjunct the Lot. Of lesser importance are aspects to the Lot and the configuration of the Lot's ruler to the Lot.

To clarify the calculation of the Lots, we shall take the Lot of Marriage as an example. This Lot is calculated by measuring the zodiacal distance from Saturn to Venus for a male and from Venus to Saturn for a female. We measure the shorter distance between the two and then based on the direction of the measurement add the distance to the Ascendant if measured in a counter-clockwise direction or subtract it from the Ascendant if measured in a clockwise direction.

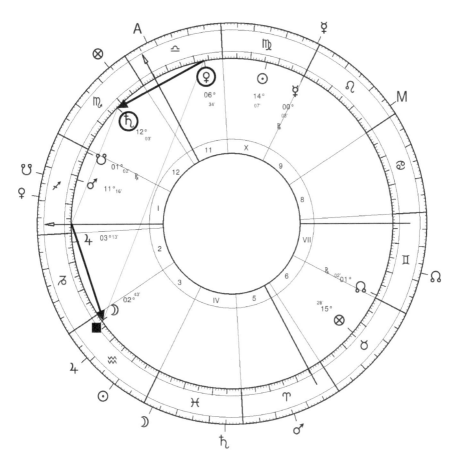

In the female horoscope above the distance from Venus to Saturn is approximately 36 degrees. **We are measuring in an anti-clockwise direction, therefore we will add the same distance to the Ascendant, going anti-clockwise.** By doing this we arrive at 3 degrees of Aquarius. This is the degree where the Lot of Marriage is (black square). In terms of geometry, the lot is a balancing point, because it brings the three points (two planets and the Ascendant) into equilibrium. The four points then form a perfect, symmetrical trapezoid. Number 4 is the number of manifestation, where polar opposites exist in space, therefore it can be understood that the Lots are points of concrete, specific manifestations.

The most widely used of all the Lots is the **Lot of Fortune** (henceforward Fortune). Its position is determined by measuring the distance from the in-sect luminary to the out-of-sect luminary and then the distance is added to, or subtracted from the Ascendant's degree. Ancient astrologers considered this Lot to be as potent as the Ascendant, therefore we shall always see if it bears additional testimony. In the horoscopes in this book Fortune will be marked with ⊗.

In the examples in this book I will always calculate the Lots manually, taking only the degrees into the account, because I have seen that the exact degree and minute are not important unless the Lot falls on a cusp. Also, unless we have all of the Lots calculated precisely by software, a calculation based only on degrees is enough for accurate results.

A very practical method of determining the positions of the Lots is by printing the horoscope in a wheel format and using a pair of compasses for measuring the distances. This is practical, fast, archaic and fun! For this reason I suggest printing the horoscopes and measuring in this way. The printed charts will also be very handy when we proceed to the examples.

6. Dignity

Throughout this book we will avoid focusing on the dignity of the planets, because I feel this is one of the most misunderstood concepts in astrology. The sole fact that there are so many different ways of assessing dignity can make one doubtful about it. We will only take into the account the universally accepted domicile rulership, exaltation and debilitation. I suggest we think about the relationship of a planet to a sign in terms of familiarity rather than dignity, because we tend to consider "dignified" malefics as less harmful, but we can ask ourselves what kind of Mars is more cruel – in his domicile / exaltation or in his fall / detriment (if one accepts detriment as legit).

CHAPTER 2
ANNUAL PROFECTIONS

1. Definition

No timing method was as widespread in various branches of ancient astrology as annual profections were. It appears they were present already in the earliest strata of Hellenistic tradition and they even appear in the famous Indian text Brihat Parashara Hora Shastra as well as the Chandrakala Nadi. The Latin word *profectio* has various meanings such as going away, setting out, departure or advance. All of these appropriately describe what happens at the turn of the native's year – departing from one sign and advancing to the next. As mentioned in the preface of this book, the principle of profections is a very simple one:

1 sign = 1 month

Each zodiacal sign represents one Solar month. Twelve Solar months constitute one Solar year. Imagine a clock and the movement of the hour and minute pointers. When the minute pointer makes a full circle the hour pointer moves to the next hour, traveling 30 degrees in the circle. When one cycle of twelve zodiacal signs is completed, the year moves to the next sign. For this reason, we can say that the following is also true:

1 sign = 1 year

Less common, but nonetheless present in the ancient traditions was the equating of one sign with a period of 2.5 days. While this is sound in theory, it has very little practical value, because as we will see in the following chapters, the determining of the month of the event is an art in itself, let alone determining the day. Most classical astrologers used only annual profections and resorted to other timing methods in order to make their forecasts more precise. Below is a table that shows how the twelve places, starting with the Ascendant are activated at particular ages.

ASC	II.	III.	IV.	V.	VI.	VII.	VIII.	IX.	X.	XI.	XII.
0	1	2	3	4	5	6	7	8	9	10	11
12	13	14	15	16	17	18	19	20	21	22	23
24	25	26	27	28	29	30	31	32	33	34	35
36	37	38	39	40	41	42	43	44	45	46	47
48	49	50	51	52	53	54	55	56	57	58	59
60	61	62	63	64	65	66	67	68	69	70	71
72	73	74	75	76	77	78	79	80	81	82	83
84	85	86	87	88	89	90	91	92	93	94	95
96	97	98	99	100	101	102	103	104	105	106	107

2. Transmissions and the ruler of the year

The most popular approach to profections is to focus on the place (house) of the profection and its ruler who becomes **the ruler of the year**. If the sign of profection is the sign of the 2nd place, then it is assumed that the theme of the year will be related to the topics of the 2nd place such as finances. Vettius Valens however, introduced a concept of **transmissions** by which the profected point or planet is said to transmit its power to the planet that rules the profection sign (the ruler of the year) and to any other planet that is **in** the sign. In my experience this is more important than the place itself, although the place is of primary importance if a planet is **in** the sign of profection, and is of secondary importance if the sign is empty.

In addition to profecting the Ascendant, Valens instructs us to profect all planets and points. Here the concept of transmission plays an important role. For example, if the annual profection of the Sun comes to Sagittarius, then it is said that the Sun transmits to Jupiter. Note that performing profections of all planets can bring out too much possibly contradictory information for an astrologer to read. Therefore it is useful to profect only the planets or points that are relevant to the topics the profection of the Ascendant is suggesting as the focus of that year. The use of these additional profections will be illustrated in chapters 5-8.

3. Setting up a context – the cycle ruler

Since the cycle of profections repeats every twelve years there need to be factors that make the cycles different from one another. Most commonly it is thought that we should look at transits and Solar returns in order to see what the difference between the same profection in two different cycles will be. While this is certainly true and should not be neglected it is nevertheless useful to establish a context. Astrologer Mohammad Imran[5] has proposed assigning the rulership of each of the 12-year cycles to one of the seven planets in the so-called ascending Chaldean order, starting with the Moon and ending with Saturn. The following table shows the planetary rulership of the 12-year cycles which create a contextual background for each cycle of annual profections.

AGE	RULER
0-11	☽
12-23	☿
24-35	♀
36-47	☉
48-59	♂
60-71	♃
72-83	♄

This concept is very similar to Ptolemy's 'ages of man'[6], but here each planet governs a time period of twelve years. Ptolemy assigned specific time periods to the planets which correspond to the natural progress of human life. While the twelve year cycles assigned to seven planets differ from the time periods given by Ptolemy, we can nevertheless see a correlation between these cycles and the progress of our lives. We could say that the cycle of the Moon is a cycle of nourishment and growth, both physical and emotional. In this cycle one is more dependent on the Mother than in any other cycle. In the cycle of Mercury we sharpen our intellect, our skills, we have a greater variety of social interactions and our body starts to take its final form. In the cycle of Venus we mature sexually and it is in this cycle that most people get married. In the cycle of the Sun we establish our authority and power and our identity is fully formed. In the cycle of Mars we continue with actions that spring from our established identity. Many people also build their second home, leaving the old one to their children, and it is usually in this cycle that we encounter more serious health problems. In the cycle of Jupiter we have had enough life experiences to become wise. It is also the time appropriate to transition from the material to the transcendental. The last is the cycle of Saturn, the time of detachment. In this cycle many souls leave their earthly bodies, or remain alone without their life-long partners, their bodies dry up and they face the inevitable decay brought by time. The ones that survive past the cycle of Saturn again come to the cycle of the Moon, where they are cared for by others almost like children and many of the "rules" don't apply to them anymore. While these kind of correlations can of course be subjective, I have found these cycles to be very valuable.

CHAPTER 3
SOLAR RETURNS

1. Significance of Solar returns

As the name implies, a Solar return is the moment when the Sun returns to the exact degree, minute and second as it was at the time of birth. A horoscope is created for this time and this is what we call a Solar return chart.

While the natal, or the root chart shows us the various themes that will unfold in the native's life, Solar returns modify these themes, even amplify them and can give us a clearer insight into what a particular year will bring. A natal chart carries within itself all of the Solar returns till the end of the native's life. Contemplating this and looking at how Solar returns link with the natal chart in the years when important events take place can evoke a great sense of awe towards the Great Mind of the universe.

The Sun, being self-illumined represents consciousness and therefore also vision, the most powerful way for the consciousness to experience the manifested reality. When the transiting Sun is at the exact natal position, the Moon and the rest of the planets who are only the reflectors of the Sun's light impress their configuration on the native through the Sun's gateway. They are the agents that carry out the mission outlined by the Sun.

2. Methodology for reading Solar returns

Different astrologers, ancient, modern and everything in between have done their best to create a methodology for reading Solar returns, from the simplest form of Solar returns of 1st century CE astrologer Dorotheus of Sidon, to mathematically complex approaches of medieval Perso-Arabic astrologer Abu Ma'shar, the later medieval Tajika system which blended Perso-Arabic and Indian concepts, all the way to renaissance French astrologer Jean-Baptiste Morin. While all of these approaches might be valid and work well for those that utilize them, I have found the Dorothean approach, where one uses a Solar return only as a set of transits to the natal chart to be a bit too simple and unreliable, while the mathematically complex approaches of the later astrologers can be very unpractical in a real-life horoscope readings unless supported by suitable computer software. These complex approaches also give an astrologer too much information to work with which can be counter-productive. Since I've been striving for a simpler approach to astrology which is mostly based on whole-sign houses and whole-sign aspects, and because I desired cohesiveness, it was natural for me to part from these complex methods. In my practice I saw how certain traditional rules for reading Solar return charts do not apply consistently. I was especially surprised to discover that the sign of annual profection, even though emphasized by many astrologers is not as important in a Solar return chart as is usually thought. Actually, putting too much focus on the profection sign can mislead us. The ruler of the year on the other hand, is extremely important as are other significators from the natal chart which repeat or confirm the natal theme in the Solar return. This of course is congruent with the approach of Abu Ma'shar, but I have decided to omit much of this method's complexity which gives too many symbols to interpret, thus no use of primary directions, 9th parts, 12th parts or quadrant house cusps within a Solar return. Instead, we shall approach a Solar return in a similar way we approach a natal chart when we use whole-sign houses or places and whole-sign aspects. Instead of mathematically complex timing techniques, we shall utilize profections, the most simple, but outstanding time-lord method.

An important thing to remember is to never read a Solar return as a standalone chart. It is fully dependent on the natal chart, the root. A Solar return can only speak about that which is already indicated in the root chart, therefore not everything is important in a Solar return. We shall now clearly lay out the methodology for approaching Solar returns that is based on my extensive empirical observations and is compliant with the principles and doctrines of classical Hellenistic astrology.

In this book we will follow these guidelines for approaching a Solar return chart:

1. Look where the ruler of the year is (the ruler of the sign of annual profection). What is its condition? Does it confirm some of the themes suggested by annual profection? Does it modify them in any way for good or bad? Is it joined or aspected by a relevant significator?

2. Look if there are any planets at the angles – Ascendant, Descendant, MC or IC. These planets are busy, loudly expressed and indicate an important year.

3. Look at relevant places and their rulers. Are they configured to the Ascendant, its ruler, some other angle, a relevant Lot or ruler of the year?

4. Look for any kind of repetition from the natal chart that is relevant for the yearly theme.

5. Planets carry their natal significations into the Solar return chart, thus if a planet rules the 7th place in the natal chart in a 7th place profection year and is at the Ascendant in the Solar return, take this as a significant indication for relationships, even if this planet rules other houses in the Solar return.

6. Look at the cycle ruler (from chapter 2), its placement and its relationship to the rest of the chart.

7. Since we are reading a Solar return, the Sun's placement and his aspects might be thought of as highly important, but in practice I've seen that the Sun as the creator of the Solar return chart is more of a passive observer. The planets joining the Sun become prominent (even if combust), but the Sun's placement is not of primary importance in regards to the main theme of the year, which came as a great surprise to me.

This approach will become more clear as we will examine 20 horoscopes in chapters 5 – 9. All Solar return charts will be cast for the birth place, in tropical zodiac, with whole-sign houses and not precessed.

CHAPTER 4
DETERMINING THE MONTH

1. Monthly profections

While the annual profection and Solar return point out the most important themes of the native's year, narrowing the window to see when a particular theme will manifested and when concrete events could take place is much more cumbersome. One way of doing this is with monthly profections. The principle is the same as with annual profections, only that we move the profected Ascendant one sign forward each month. Therefore, if the profected Ascendant is in Leo, then Leo is also the first month of the native's year. We then move forward one sign per month and come full circle back to Leo. At that point the annual profection of course moves forward to the next sign, much like how the hour pointer on a clock moves one hour forward when the minute pointer travels a full circle.

Determining the exact month of the event with monthly profections alone is difficult, because we are usually left with three choices or sometimes even more. We can assume that the event will take place when the monthly profection will be to the sign that holds the ruler of the year. Or, maybe when the profection reaches one of the two signs ruled by this planet, or maybe when it reaches some other important and relevant significator. There are usually too many options and I've found that my forecasts were accurate as often as they were wrong.

This led me to the search for a complementary timing technique that would preferably be performed in the Solar return chart and would help me to choose the month of an event more effectively. After some trial and error and a few sleepless nights I came to a very simple technique which adheres to the principle of monthly profections (1 sign = 1 month) and is performed in the Solar return chart. Since this is the first timing method that I have found to be both simple and to a large degree reliable, I have decided to share it in this book. Let's take a look at it.

2. Timing in Solar returns

This timing method will be explained in depth throughout the course of this book. At this point we shall only look at it from the conceptual and philosophical standpoint.

It is understood that the Zodiacal signs are Solar months. Since a Solar return chart is a yearly chart we can only perform monthly profections in it, thus counting signs as months. The Sun has already set up the whole Solar return chart with his return to the natal position. His reflection, the Moon as the significator of the mind-body complex through which an individualized portion of consciousness is experiencing the material reality has yet to play her part. It is for this reason that many astrologers reach for Lunar returns in order to determine the month of an event. This is certainly an effective approach, but unfortunately I find it impractical unless some indicators can lead me towards the correct month before I reach for a Lunar return. If we don't have such a tool at our disposal, then we need to look at many Lunar returns in order to know which month to focus on. With a computer software this is of course possible, but let me remind you that the purpose of this book is to present a methodology that is simple, practical and can be easily practiced without any astrology software. The only thing we need is a drawing of the natal chart and the Solar return chart for the year in question. The rest can be all done by hand. This simple but effective method is as follows:

1. In the Solar return chart determine which of the planets are the candidates to become the significator of the key event or the unfolding of the yearly theme.

2. Count how many signs the Moon needs to travel to reach each one of them. In this way we are basically profecting the Moon, so that she transmits to the candidates.

3. Determine the time period of one month suggested by the Moon's profection to these candidates.

4. Return to the natal chart and see which one of the months suggested by the Moon's profection in the Solar return is confirmed by monthly profections.

The method is very straightforward and is built on the classical principle of profection and transmission as expounded by Vettius Valens throughout his Anthology. It will become clearer through the examples in the following chapters.

CHAPTER 5
RELATIONSHIPS & MARRIAGES

1. Relevant places

In the Hellenistic tradition as well as in modern astrology the 7th place is the place of marriage. Since we are looking at the event of a wedding, we shall also take into the account the 9th place, because it is the place of God and ceremonies. We shall also consider the 3rd place, because it is the 9th from the 7th, thus ceremonies related to marriage. These two places, as we will see play an important role in the years when weddings take place.

2. Relevant planets

Venus as the goddess of love and a unifying principle is the natural significator of marriage and also weddings with their beauty, music, socializing and good food. Besides Venus there is another planet without which no oath could be taken – Saturn. Entering a marriage requires a commitment and it inevitably sets boundaries, therefore Saturn, as we will see, plays an important role in years that bring weddings.

3. Relevant Lots

Besides places and planets which can carry many different meanings, the ancient astrologers frequently calculated points or the so called Lots that represented specific, concrete things.

Dorotheus of Sidon introduced a specific **Lot of Marriage**[7] which symbolizes the element of commitment the most. As explained in chapter 1, it is calculated by taking the distance from Saturn to Venus for a male and from Venus to Saturn for a female. This distance is then added to or subtracted from the Ascendant degree. As we can see, the Lot uses the before mentioned Venus and Saturn. This Lot shall be the most important Lot to analyze when it comes to taking a marriage vow. There are, however three other Lots related to relationships which are calculated in the following ways:

1. **Lot of Wife** – distance from Sun to Venus, added to or subtracted from the Ascendant[8]
2. **Lot of Husband** – distance from Moon to Mars, added to or subtracted from the Ascendant
3. **Lot of Union** – this is a different version of the Lot of Marriage which is quite popular and was also given by Dorotheus[9]. It is calculated by taking the distance from Venus to the Descendant degree and adding it to or subtracting it from the Ascendant degree. In order to distinguish it from the Lot of Marriage I've decided to name it the Lot of Union, because its nature is a bit broader than that of the Lot of Marriage.

As we will see in the following examples these Lots and their rulers are often important factors and can help us determine which of the possible themes of a particular place will actually manifest in a given year.

4. Examples

EXAMPLE 1

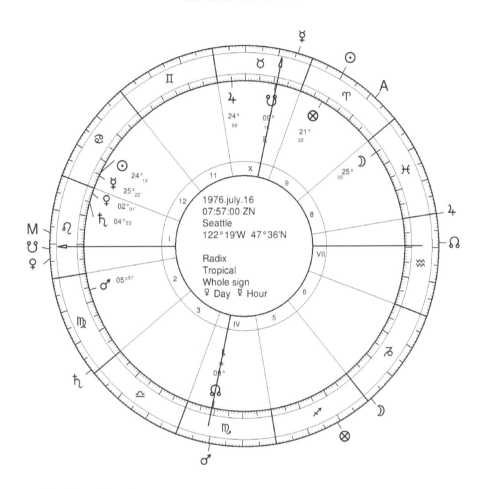

Gender: Female

Event: Wedding

Date: 7th of October, 2006

Age: 30

Cycle ruler: Venus

Profection: Aquarius / 7th place

Ruler of the year: Saturn

Expected significators: Saturn, Venus, Lot of Marriage, Lot of Union, Lot of Husband, 7th place, 9th place, 3rd place.

ANNUAL PROFECTIONS

The annual profection is to **Aquarius** which is the **7th place**. **Saturn** who rules the year is **in the 1st place with Venus**, the natural significator of marriage and the ruler of the **3rd place**. Since we already have two marriage significators active, we shall look at the relevant Lots. The **Lot of Marriage** is at 23 degrees of Leo and the **Lot of Husband** is at 1 degree of Aquarius, thus two relevant Lots are activated.

If we profect the ruler of the year Saturn, he transmits to himself in the 7th place. Likewise, by profecting Venus as the cycle ruler and marriage significator we arrive to the 7th place and transmission to Saturn. Additionally, Fortune profects to Libra and thus transmits to Venus. At this point we can be certain that the theme of marriage will be an important theme of this year.

SOLAR RETURN

In the Solar return chart the ruler of the year **Saturn** is in the auspicious 11th place, in-sect and **co-present with Mars who rules the 7th place and is conjunct the Lot of Union** (27 degrees of Leo). Additionally, Saturn also rules the Solar return Ascendant by exaltation. **The Moon is in the 7th place**, received by Mars with a trine aspect. Mars is in an exact trine with the Descendant and aspects Venus with a sextile. **Venus** is in the **9th** place, in an exact sextile to the Descendant and Mars. It is important to note that Mars rules the 9th place in the natal chart, while Saturn rules the 7th. They have joined together in Leo in this Solar return, and it is this sign (Leo) that Saturn occupies in the natal chart. Mercury, the 9th ruler and ruler of Venus, is retrograde and conjunct the Sun while the Moon who rules Cancer is in the 7th, aspecting Cancer with a square. The themes of relationship and ceremony are beautifully tied together.

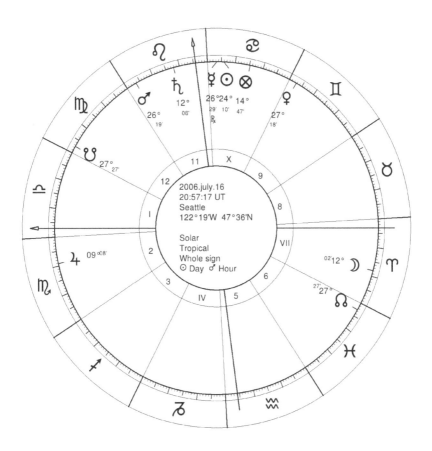

TIMING THE THEME IN THE SOLAR RETURN

As proposed in chapter 4, we shall now choose the significator that will highlight the month in which the theme could unfold the most. In this chart we can choose the most important significator between these candidates:

1. Mars and Saturn who are trine to the 7th
2. Venus, who is in the 9th and sextile to both Mars and the Descendant

Mars and Saturn are both malefics. While Saturn is very relevant for a wedding as it binds the two persons together and sets up boundaries, Mars, apart from ruling the 7th is not a symbol particularly suitable for a wedding.

Venus, a benefic, in the 9th and aspecting both the 7th ruler Mars and the Descendant so tightly shall be our first choice, especially due to her presence in the 1st house in the natal chart.

Now, that we have selected the significator, we shall profect the Moon and see how many signs she needs to move through in order to get to the sign where Venus is. From Aries to Gemini are three signs (Aries counts as the first sign/month), thus the theme could unfold most likely in the 3rd month of the native's year, which is the period between the 16th of September and 16th of October.

MONTHLY PROFECTIONS

Up to this point we have narrowed down the possible themes suggested by the natal chart with the use of the Solar return chart and concluded that marriage is the main focus of the year. Profection of the Moon in the Solar return chart has suggested that the theme will most likely unfold in the period between the 16th of September and 16th of October. Now we can go back to the natal chart and perform monthly profections in order to see if any of the months indicated by the profected Moon in the Solar return will be confirmed.

We will start counting the months from the sign of annual profection which is Aquarius. Counting three signs brings us to Aries, the 9th place. Aries holds Fortune, but also the *dodekatemoria* of the Sun and the Ascendant. Mars as the ruler of the 9th is in the 2nd, which does not speak in favor of a wedding, however, because of the importance of the *dodekatemoria*, as seen in chapter 1, the *dodekatemoria* of the Sun and the Ascendant should not be taken too lightly. Here we have the *dodekatemorion* of the Ascendant and its ruler in the 9th place of ceremonies. It is very important to keep in mind, that we are using the monthly profections only to see if our timing from the Solar return chart is being confirmed. In this case, we can definitely say yes, because the wedding took place in the third month, on the **7th of October** in the period suggested by our timing method in the Solar return chart.

EXAMPLE 2

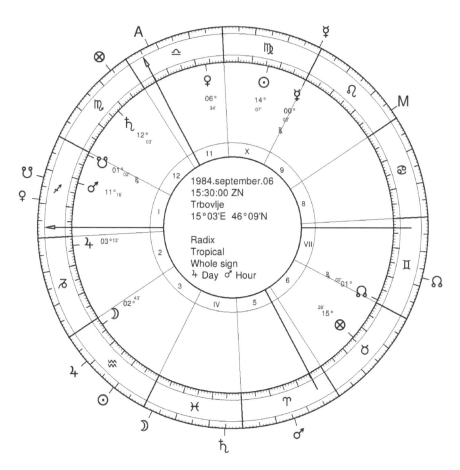

Gender: Female

Event: Wedding

Date: 29th of May, 2019

Age: 34

Cycle ruler: Venus

Profection: Libra / 11th place

Ruler of the year: Venus

Expected significators: Venus, Mercury, Lot of Marriage, Lot of Union, Lot of Husband, 7th place, 9th place, 3rd place.

ANNUAL PROFECTIONS

The annual profection sign is **Libra**, therefore **Venus rules the year**. She is in her own sign Libra and by her *dodekatemorion* in the 1ˢᵗ place. Libra in turn holds the *dodekatermorion* of the Ascendant, thus we should pay attention to this link between Venus and the Ascendant, the native and topics symbolized by Venus, such as love, romance, beauty and marriage. Since she is in Libra, the sign of relationships and in the auspicious 11ᵗʰ place, the year is most likely relationship centered, with a fair amount of good luck in terms of both social interactions and prosperity.

If we profect the cycle and year ruler Venus she transmits to the Sun and arguably to retrograde Mercury who rules the 7ᵗʰ and 10ᵗʰ place, on the Leo/Virgo cusp, moving out of Sun's beams and entering back into the 9ᵗʰ place. Fitting to Mercury's condition, the native was married to a foreigner of a different race in a foreign land. Venus is aspecting the 7ᵗʰ place with a trine, Mars with a sextile and is dominating Jupiter through a square aspect. Interestingly enough, the **Lot of Union** is at 17 degrees of Virgo, just 3 degrees from the Sun to whom Venus transmits. A relationship in a far away land is indicated again as a theme with the Sun being in the 12ᵗʰ place from Venus.

At this point we need to look at the Solar return chart in order to get a clearer idea of what exactly is unfolding in this year. It might be an important step in a relationship, a friendship, or even just some material gain from her work. We could also see a certain amount of loss and grief, because Saturn, the exaltation ruler of Libra is in the 12ᵗʰ place of bad spirit and in Scorpio.

This was certainly so, because the native relocated to a far away land with a very different culture and this transition was not easy.

SOLAR RETURN

The ruler of the year **Venus is in the 7ᵗʰ place in Libra**, very close to the Descendant. The chart is nocturnal, thus Venus is even more beneficial.

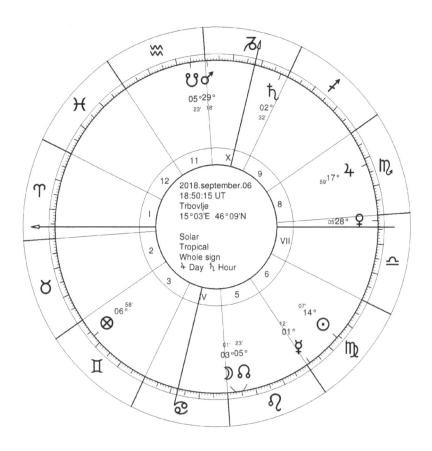

The Ascendant ruler Mars, who also rules the **Lot of Union** (24 degrees of Aries) is exalted in the 10ᵗʰ place and square to Venus and the Ascendant. He is advancing towards the MC, therefore he is strongly expressed. Since he is the in-sect malefic, exalted and strong, a possible bold step related to the 7th house topics could be undertaken that would most likely have a stable long term effect (movable earth sign). The importance of Venus increases even more with her rulership over the **Lot of Husband** which is at 22 degrees of Libra, very close to the Descendant.

Saturn also has some importance, although he is not a time-lord in this year. He is in the 10th place in his own domicile and he rules the **Lot of Marriage** at 22 degrees of Aquarius.

The Moon is with the North Node in the 5th place, possibly indicating a sudden, unusual and unexpected romance. She is in a square with Jupiter who rules the 9th place of travel, foreign lands and ceremonies, which indicates that the native will take sudden action towards romance, possibly related to a foreign land or a foreigner. Due to square aspect being challenging there is bound to be some stress involved, too. The Moon is also in a sextile to Venus, showing good fortune in regards to marriage.

TIMING THE THEME IN THE SOLAR RETURN

In this Solar Return chart we shall choose the most suitable significator among these candidates:

1. Venus in the 7$^{th.}$
2. Mars in Capricorn
3. The Ascendant

Venus is of course a very clear candidate, because she rules the year and is properly placed.

Regarding Mars we have two options. The first is Capricorn, but we also have Saturn there, who in this chart is not associated with marriage, but does rule the 3rd place in the natal chart. The second option is Aries, the rising sign. This would activate the 1st / 7th axis more and also activate Mars on its own more, as well as his square aspect to Venus.

Now, let us count signs from the Moon to Venus. The distance is 3 signs, thus suggesting the 3rd month of the native's year, which is the period from the 6th of November to 6th of December.

From the Moon to the Ascendant, our third candidate is 9 signs, suggesting the 9th month, which is the period from the 6th of May to 6th of June.

MONTHLY PROFECTIONS

Now, let us go back to the natal chart and perform monthly profections from Libra which is the sign of annual profection. Counting 3 signs brings us to Sagittarius, the 1st place, which holds the *dodekatemorion* of Venus.

Counting 9 signs from Libra brings us to Gemini, the 7th place and activates Mercury, which, as we have seen earlier hints towards unusual marriage and foreign places. The monthly profection to Gemini gives the correct picture, because the native got married on the **29th of May**, thus in the period suggested by the Moon's profection to the Ascendant in the Solar return chart.

It is intriguing that none of the relevant Lots were very clearly activated in this year apart from the Lot of Union in Virgo, which due to retrograde Mercury's placement on the cusp cannot be overly relied upon. On the other hand, the Lot of Marriage is in Aquarius, ruled by Saturn who is in the 12th place. However, Saturn can be considered a co-ruler of the year, because he exalts in Libra. The native has settled in a marriage in a far away land and she had to let go of almost everything she had.

EXAMPLE 3

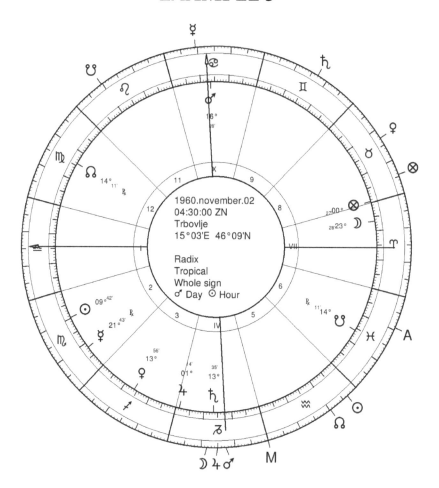

Gender: Female

Event: Wedding

Date: 10th of March, 1979

Age: 18

Cycle ruler: Mercury

Profection: Aries / 7th place

Ruler of the year: Mars, the Moon

Expected significators: The Moon, Mars, Venus, Lot of Marriage, Lot of Union, Lot of Husband, 7th, 9th, 3rd place.

ANNUAL PROFECTIONS

The annual profection sign is **Aries, the 7th place**, thus the Moon and Mars can be considered co-rulers of the year. They are in a square aspect and a mutual reception which mitigates Mars's debilitation. He is also very strong at the MC. If we profect the Moon, she profects to Libra and thus **transmits to Venus,** and if we profect the cycle ruler Mercury, the transmission is **to Venus** through Taurus, where she also has her *dodekatemorion*. Venus is in the **3rd place** of marriage ceremonies. Lastly, by profection Mars transmits to Saturn in Capricorn where the **Lot of Husband** is located (7 degrees of Capricorn). By now we already have some good indications that a marriage could take place in this year, but let's look at the other relevant lots also. The **Lot of Marriage** is at 14 degrees of Scorpio**, ruled by Mars**. This further highlights the theme of marriage, but can also make us consider Mars's placement in the 10th place and Saturn's opposition to him. The native chose to cease with education in favor of marriage and children, and thus took an important decision regarding her future career. Let us now proceed and take a look at the Solar return chart for this year.

SOLAR RETURN

The Moon and Mars who are important players in the radix chart **are conjunct at the MC**, at the beginning of the 11th place of Good Spirit, gain and also one of the two houses of children. It might be appropriate to state that the native was pregnant at this time. The ruler of the MC and the 11th place Jupiter is in the 7th **place**, strongly advancing towards the Descendant and is in sect. Mars at the MC rules the **3ʳᵈ place** and the **Lot of Marriage** (11 degrees of Aries), so his presence at the MC and conjunction with the Moon gains even more importance.

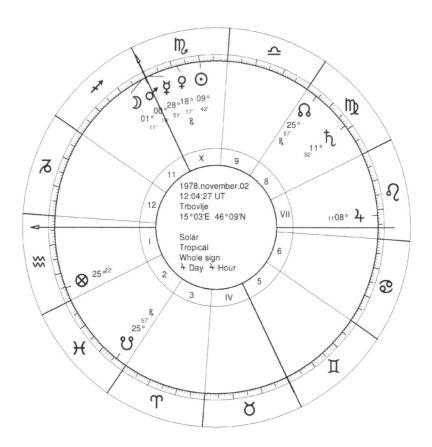

Although Venus is not activated as a time-lord in this year it is still worth paying attention to her, because she is nevertheless the natural significator of marriage and in this Solar return she rules the **9ᵗʰ place** and the **Lot of Union** (10 degrees of Libra). She is retrograde and 8 degrees from the Sun, thus under his beams. I have seen that the important planets in Solar returns are often retrograde, combust, or both.

Saturn, the Ascendant ruler and ruler of Fortune is in the difficult 8th place, amplified by the North Node. While the topic of marriage seems to be favored by this year's placements, there is nevertheless some difficulty with the body indicated, and possibly a danger of death, especially because Mercury as the ruler of the 8th is conjunct Mars at the MC. The native did go through a serious health issues connected to her pregnancy. Since we are concerned with marital affairs, we shall now again focus on the wedding significators and the timing of the theme.

TIMING THE THEME IN THE SOLAR RETURN

In this Solar return chart the significator can be chosen among these candidates:

1. Mars, who is conjunct the Moon
2. Jupiter, who is in the 7th

Mars, being the 3rd ruler and also the ruler of the 7th in the natal chart is a good candidate. He is received by Jupiter, who is in the 7th place. Jupiter of course is a good candidate, because he rules the Moon and Mars. Taking the 1st month due to the Moon being conjunct Mars would be reasonable, but the 11th place itself is not indicative enough for a wedding.

Let's profect the Moon to Aries, 3rd place so that she transmits to Mars and arrives to the place of ceremonies related to marriage. From the Moon to Aries is 5 signs, indicating the 5th month of the native's year which is the period between the 2nd of March and 2nd of April.

MONTHLY PROFECTIONS

By counting 5 signs from the annual profection sign Aries in the natal chart we arrive to Leo, 11th place. Leo does not hold any relevant significator, therefore we shall look at the Sun's placement. The Sun is in Scorpio, with the 9th ruler Mercury, both co-present with Lot of Marriage, thus in the place of marriage according to Firmicus Maternus[10]. The native got married on the **10th of March**, which is in the period suggested by the timing in the Solar return chart.

While we might opt for another sign or place, for example Cancer or Sagittarius if we'd select the month without the help of the Solar return chart, it is the Solar return that defines the month, and monthly profections in the natal chart only serve as a confirmation tool.

EXAMPLE 4

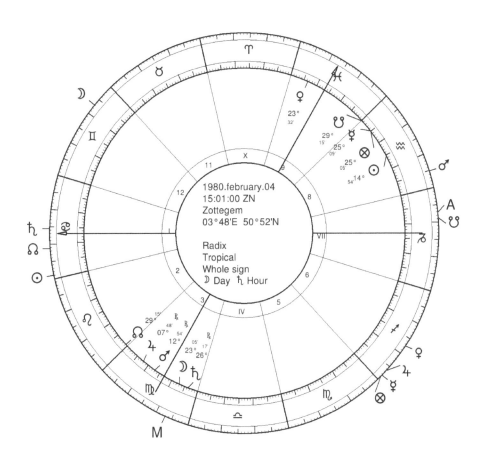

Gender: Male

Event: Wedding

Date: 12th of October, 2019

Age: 39

Cycle ruler: The Sun

Profection: Libra / 4th place

Ruler of the year: Venus

Expected significators: Venus, Jupiter, Saturn, Lot of Marriage, Lot of Union, Lot of Wife, 7th place, 9th place, 3rd place.

ANNUAL PROFECTIONS

The ruler of the year **Venus is exalted in the 9th place**, strongly advancing towards the MC, which immediately makes us pay attention to Venus and the possibility of either a wedding or travel to a foreign country due to Venus ruling the 4th place and being placed in the 9th. She also rules the **Lot of Union** which is at 11 degrees of Taurus. **Jupiter**, her ruler is in the **3rd place**, which as we have seen is a place connected to weddings. He is co-present with the Moon who rules the Ascendant and with the 7th ruler Saturn who also rules the **Lot of Marriage** (14 degrees of Capricorn). The native married a woman from a foreign country and the wedding took place in a foreign country, too. In addition, if we profect the cycle ruler **the Sun and Fortune**, they transmit **to Venus**, affirming the importance of Venus in this year.

SOLAR RETURN

The ruler of the year **Venus** has just entered **Capricorn, the 3rd place**. She is the benefic of the sect as the chart is nocturnal. She is there with Saturn who rules the 3rd place. Furthermore, she is the ruler of the 7th place, which creates a clear connection between 3rd and 7th places, something we would want to see when predicting a wedding. It might be interesting to add that Venus also rules the 12th place and that their wedding was held in secrecy. Furthermore, the **Lot of Wife** is in the 12th place at 11 degrees of Libra, connecting spouse and secrecy with the 3rd place of wedding ceremonies.

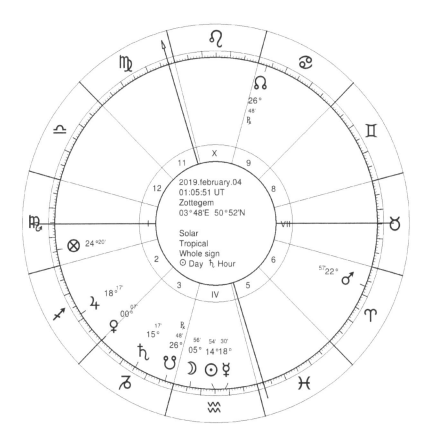

A curious thing is **the Ascendant ruler Mars** is in the 6th place, thus in the 12th from the 7th which we could associate with hurdles in marriage instead of a wedding. But Mars is joyful in the 6th place, he is in his domicile and in sect, which makes him less malefic. He rules the **Lot of Union** (0 degrees Aries), tying the Ascendant with the relevant lot, albeit in the difficult 6th place. We should note that such a Mars is fully masculine and overcomes the obstacles and enemies (6th place) by taking the right action.

TIMING THE THEME IN THE SOLAR RETURN

In this Solar return chart we can choose the significator among these candidates:

1. Venus, who rules the year and the 7th place
2. Moon, who rules the 7th by exaltation and the 9th

The Moon is in the 4th place as the 9th ruler, thus more indicative of changing countries and travel. Venus, however is perfectly placed to indicate a wedding ceremony.

For timing the unfolding of the theme we have three options. The first one is to profect the Moon to Taurus, the 7th place and thus activate the 7th place and Venus in the 3rd. The second option is to profect the Moon to Libra, which is the 12th place from the Ascendant and the 9th place from the Moon. This would activate Venus primarily as the 12th ruler in the 3rd, which could also be fitting, since the wedding ceremony was held in secrecy, but without knowing this most astrologers would probably prefer the Moon's profecton to Taurus or even to Capricorn, so that she would transmit to both Venus and Saturn.

Profecting the Moon to Taurus suggests the 4th month, thus the period between the 4th of May and 4th of June. Profecting her to Libra suggests the 9th month which is the period between the 4th of October and 4th of November. Lastly, profecting the Moon to Capricorn suggests the 12th month which is the period between the 4th of January and 4th of February.

MONTHLY PROFECTIONS

In the natal chart, counting 4 signs from Libra brings us to Capricorn, the 7th place, which is very appropriate and self explanatory.

Counting 9 signs from Libra brings us to Gemini, the 12th place, which at first doesn't look promising, but, Mercury is conjunct Fortune and rules the 3rd place, which is the most important place for a wedding in this horoscope, as it holds two crucial significators (Saturn and the Moon – rulers of the 1st and the 7th). The only downside to Mercury is that it's in the 8th place and thus in aversion to both, Venus and Saturn. It is important to notice that the aversion to Saturn is mitigated by their mutual reception. If we pay attention to the *dodekatemoria*, we can see that Mercury's *dodekatemorion* is co-present with those of Venus and Jupiter, thus their aversion is no longer true, either. Gemini, the sign in question also holds the *dodekatemorion* of the Moon, thus activating the Moon in the 3rd place. While this might seem like a whole lot of unnecessary astro-gymnastics to some, we have been cautioned by Firmicus Maternus to always pay attention to the *dodekatemoria* in order to not be mislead in our judgment of a horoscope.

Lastly, counting 12 signs from Libra brings us to Virgo, the 3rd place, which directs our attention to another very appropriate set of symbols, due to the important significators being situated therein.

The selection of the significator in this example is difficult. While many astrologers would probably choose monthly profection to

Virgo as it is a double-bodied sign and the 3rd place, some might want to see the ruler of the 3rd place to be activated, too. This creates a need for an additional step in timing, which can help us find the correct month.

As a fun exercise we can perform additional monthly profections from the cycle ruler and sect light, the Sun. Vettius Valens instructs us to profect all planets and points, but let us do this only with the truly relevant significators. Moving the Sun forward 4 signs as this is the 4th place profection year brings us to Taurus, as we have seen earlier. By profection the Sun transmits to Venus, which is appropriate for the theme we're concerned with. Here we can ask ourselves in which of the available months would the Sun profect monthly to either Gemini, Virgo or Capricorn which are our signs of choice. The Sun profects monthly to Capricorn in the 9th month. This is the only month where he transmits to one of the relevant significators, to Saturn, ruler of the 7th who is situated in the 3rd place. This secret wedding indeed took place in the 9th month of the native's year, on the **12th of October**, thus in the period between the 4th of October and 4th of November.

As we have seen, not all horoscopes speak clearly right away when it comes to predicting a theme or an event to the month. In some cases a more detailed and involved work is necessary and of course more meditation and even a greater use of our intuition which highlights the important symbols in the horoscope we are examining.

EXAMPLE 5

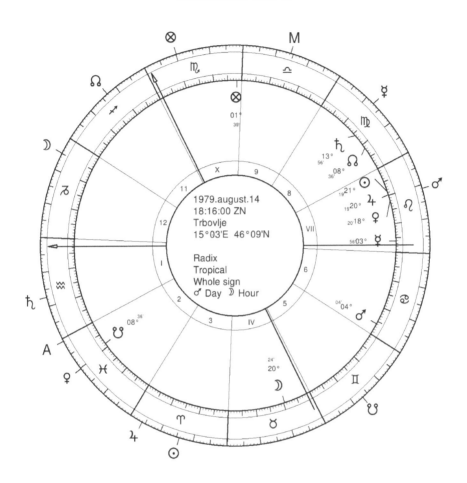

Gender: Male

Event: First date with his future wife

Date: 3rd of June, 2002

Age: 22

Cycle ruler: Mercury

Profection: Sagittarius / 11th place

Ruler of the year: Jupiter

Expected significators: Jupiter, Venus, Mercury, Lot of Wife (partner), Lot of Union, 7th place, 5th place, 11th place.

ANNUAL PROFECTIONS

The annual profection is to **Sagittarius, the 11th place** making **Jupiter the ruler of the year.** He is in the **7th place** conjunct the Sun who is the 7th ruler and Venus, the significator of love. Jupiter is within 1 degree of the Sun both in longitude and lattitude which some ancient authors such as Rhetorius would consider as *cazimi* or being in the heart of the Sun, thus no longer combust[11]. Venus on the other hand is clearly in a deep combustion, thus Jupiter can bring more benefit to the 7th place than Venus can. This said, Venus is exalted by her *dodekatemorion* and in practice it can be observed that combustion is not always destructive. Jupiter is also the benefic of the sect. There is good spirit, good luck and an increase flowing towards the area of relationships.

The cycle ruler **Mercury is strong at the Descendant** and just free of the Sun's rays. It rules the 8th place, thus ruling over Saturn who is the Ascendant ruler and represents the native. Mercury also rules topics of enjoyment, romance and love as the 5th ruler. The 8th place deserves to be mentioned as positive here, because the native inherited an apartment in that year, which is indicated by Mercury's (8th ruler) co-presence with Venus, the 4th ruler.

If we profect the Leo stellium, which includes the Sun as the 7th ruler, Venus as the significator of love, Jupiter as the benefic of the sect and the 11th ruler, and Mercury (the cycle ruler) we get to Gemini, the 5th place of romance and thus back to Mercury in the 7th place.

Let us proceed with analyzing the Solar return chart of this year in order to get a clearer picture of what type of a 7th house related event might actually take place.

SOLAR RETURN

The first thing we notice is **Venus rising** in a nocturnal horoscope. She is tightly conjunct the Ascendant, therefore she is very strong and significant.

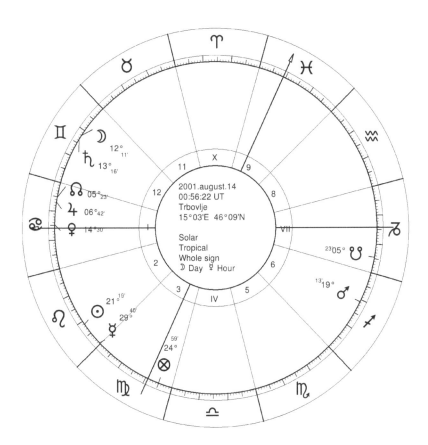

The exalted ruler of the year Jupiter has already risen, and is with the North Node, the amplifier of his significations and the bringer of sudden new things. The ruler of the 7th, Saturn is conjunct the Moon who rules the Ascendant, bringing the topic of relationship to the native. At this point it has to be mentioned that while the year was for the most part positive there was also an onset of an unidentified health problem, which the Moon's conjunction with Saturn in the 12th place illustrates nicely. Here we can see how one set of symbols speak about two experiences of a vastly different nature, depending on the context. While the 12th place seems inappropriate for such a romantic event a revelation of an important detail might help to clarify this. The romance started with long, secluded spiritual and psychological talks in the woods, sharing each other's fears, sorrows and spiritual experiences. Interestingly enough, the Lot of Wife (in this case girlfriend) is at 7 degrees of Gemini, conjunct the Moon, who rules the Ascendant. Symbolically the native joins with the other (Saturn as the 7th ruler) and their union is very much isolated and hidden from the eyes of society. Both of them were loners at that time and the new girlfriend had pronounced Saturnian traits.

TIMING THE THEME IN THE SOLAR RETURN

In this Solar Return chart we can select the significator among these candidates:

1. Saturn, who is conjunct the Moon
2. Venus, who is conjunct the Ascendant
3. Jupiter, who is exalted in the 1st and rules the year

While Saturn rules the 7th, his conjunction with the Moon, the 1st ruler is happening in the 12th place which is not a place we would associate with falling in love, apart from it being the place of bed pleasures according to some astrologers. Saturn there, however, would not indicate pleasures, therefore we can rule out Saturn as being a suitable significator.

Venus and Jupiter are both appropriate and thus we have two choices for profecting the Moon. The first is to profect Venus to Cancer, which would suggest the 2nd month of the native's year which is from the 14th of September to 14th of October 2001. The second option is to profect the Moon to the MC in Pisces which is the domicile of Jupiter and the exaltation sign of Venus. This would activate three important significators which is desirable. The month suggested by profecting the Moon to Pisces is the 10th month, because Pisces is the 10th sign from Gemini. This suggests the period between the 14th of May and 14th of June 2002.

MONTHLY PROFECTIONS

We shall now count the months from the annual profection sign Sagittarius in the natal chart. Counting 2 signs as suggested by profecting the Moon to Cancer in Solar return brings us to Capricorn. This does not confirm the first option from Solar return, therefore we shall now try the second option. Counting 10 signs from Sagittarius brings us to Virgo, which holds the Ascendant ruler Saturn and the *dodekatemorion* of Mercury. The activation of Mercury is happening through his rulership of Virgo and his *dodekatemorion*. Because Mercury is sitting on the

Descendant and also rules the 5th place of love and romance, the 10th month seems to be suitable for the unfolding of the love theme. Indeed, the native went on the first date with his soon-to-become wife on the **3rd of July 2002**, which is the period suggested by the Solar return timing.

CHAPTER 6
CHILDBIRTH

1. Relevant places

Common to all classical astrological texts, the 5th place is considered to be the place of children. It is the 11th place as counted from the place of marriage which is the 7th place, therefore we can say that the 5th place represents gains from marriage. The most obvious gain or increase related to marriage are of course children. The other place related to children is the 11th place, being the 5th from the 7th, thus representing the children of one's spouse, or even children of other people. Since the meaning of both of these places is derived from their relationship with the 7th place, we shall take the 7th place to be relevant also, because it is the place of sexual union, where the sky meets the earth and conception takes place.

2. Relevant planets

Jupiter, the planet of luck, joy and expansion was always considered to be the significator of children and thus he shall be taken as the most important of the planets. The other significator is the Moon, being the Cosmic Mother, the Divine Feminine through whom all living beings emerge in form.

3. Relevant Lots

The Lots that signify children are the Lot of Children, the Lot of Daughters and the Lot of Sons. They are calculated in the following ways:

1. **Lot of Children 1** – distance from Jupiter to Saturn, added to or subtracted from the Ascendant degree[12].
2. **Lot of Children 2** – distance from Jupiter to the 5th equal house cusp (the same degree the Ascendant is at, but in the 5th whole-sign place), added to or subtracted from the Ascendant degree.
3. **Lot of Daughters** – distance from Jupiter to Venus, added to or subtracted from the Ascendant degree.
4. **Lot of Sons** – distance from Jupiter to Mercury, added to or subtracted from the Ascendant degreee[13].

4. Examples

EXAMPLE 1

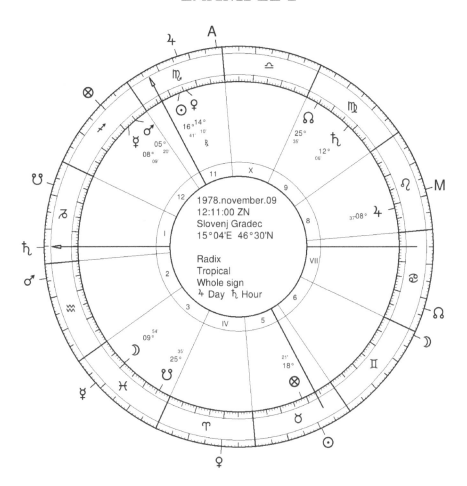

Gender: Male
Event: Birth of son
Date: 17th of December, 2012
Age: 34
Cycle ruler: Venus
Profection: Scorpio / 11th place
Ruler of the year: Venus, the Sun, Mars
Expected significators: Venus, Jupiter, Fortune, Lot of Sons, Lot of Children, 5th place, 11th place

ANNUAL PROFECTIONS

The sign of annual profection is **Scorpio**, the **11th place** (gain and children of one's spouse, good fortune from marriage) and the ruler of the year is **Mars**. The Sun and **Venus** are significant factors also, because they are in the sign of profection. Venus rules the **5th place** (children), Fortune, the **Lot of Son** (24 degrees of Taurus) and the 10th place. **She is conjunct the Lot of Children 2** which is at 12 degrees of Scorpio.

Jupiter, the significator of children and benefic of the sect, while in the 8th place and at first glance not able to give children has his *dodekatemorion* in the profection sign Scorpio, conjunct the Lot of Children 2 and Venus, therefore Venus while retrograde and combust gets influenced by Jupiter through his *dodekatemorion*. He is also in a square to Venus, thus dominating her by being in the 10th place from her. Jupiter's ruler the Sun is of course in the 11th place, receiving Jupiter by a square aspect.

The ruler of the year Mars is the out-of-sect malefic, in the unfortunate 12th place, but is in the 5th from Jupiter (affirming the theme of children) and thus in a trine aspect being received by him in Sagittarius. Jupiter is also in a superior position, being earlier in Zodiacal order, therefore Jupiter is strongly controlling Mars and is making him less maleficent.

If we profect **the cycle ruler Venus**, the profection is to Saturn, the ascendant ruler, linking Venus's agenda with the native. If we profect the ruler of the year Mars, we get to Libra and Venus, which further suggests the already established theme.

SOLAR RETURN

The ruler of the year Mars is in the 7th place and rules the 11th place which is the 5th from the 7th, thus the place of children of the spouse, which is important to consider in a male horoscope, as it is the female, the spouse that is giving birth. As we will see later though, the 11th place features prominently in female horoscopes too. Mars's ruler **Jupiter is rising**, tightly conjunct the Ascendant and is retrograde. The Ascendant ruler Mercury is in the 7th, co-present with the ruler of the year, indicating a relationship centered year.

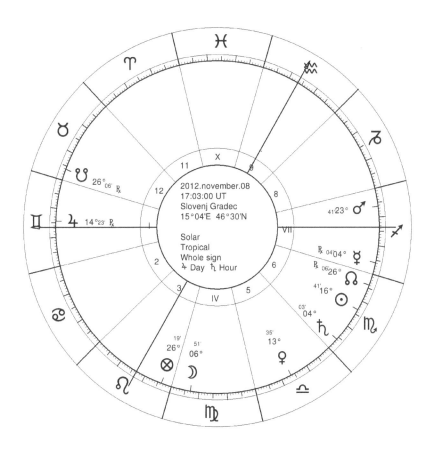

So far the year seems a bit more focused on relationships than children, but if we look at the **Lot of Sons** at 6 degrees of Gemini, in the 1st place and with Jupiter, then the topic of sons emerges. Mercury, the ruler of the Lot is with Mars who rules the year and the 11th place of the Solar return, thus we now have a flow between the 1st, 7th and 11th places, the Lot of Sons and Jupiter as the natural significator of children.

Venus is in the **5th** in her domicile of Libra, trine to the Ascendant and Jupiter. Since this is a nocturnal horoscope, Venus is extremely beneficial. There is auspiciousness related to relationships and children flowing to the native, the Ascendant. There is also harmony through a sextile aspect between Mars and Venus, rulers of the 5th and 11th places which at this point turns our attention towards the topic of children.

While the natal chart is showing a mixed year with Mars being in the 12th and being ruled by Jupiter who is in the 8th, both in difficult houses, the Solar return chart modifies this and suggests a more tempered year with the influence of benefics being stronger. It also helps us to be more certain that the themes of children and relationship would be important in this year.

TIMING THE THEME IN THE SOLAR RETURN

In this Solar return chart we can choose the most important significator among three candidates:

1. Mars, who rules the year, the 11th place and is angular

76

2. Venus, who is in the 5th in her domicile and in sect
3. Jupiter, who is on the Ascendant and is the natural significator of children

Since the horoscope is nocturnal we shall choose Venus, due to her placement being the most directly tied to the topic of children and the fact that she is not dependent on any other planet. Furthermore, she also rules the 5th in the natal chart and is placed in the 11th. Therefore she is repeating the theme that is suggested in the natal chart the most.

Mars rules the 11th in both the natal chart and Solar return. He is the in-sect malefic, so we would give preference to Venus, the benefic of the nocturnal sect.

Let us now profect the Moon and see when she transmits to the chosen significator. Venus is in the 2nd sign from the Moon, therefore the Moon transmits to Venus in the 2nd month of the native's year, thus in the period from the 8th of December and the 8th of January.

MONTHLY PROFECTIONS

In the radix chart we start counting months from Scorpio, the sign of the annual profection. By counting 2 signs we get to Sagittarius in December. Sagittarius holds Mars who rules the year and also rules Venus. This confirms what we've already seen in the Solar return chart as the native's son was born on the **17th of December**. Let us again remember that all we are using monthly profections for is to confirm what the timing method in the Solar return chart suggests, therefore all we are searching for is a suitable planet being activated. It can be activated through its placement, the sign it rules or through its *dodekatemorion*.

EXAMPLE 2

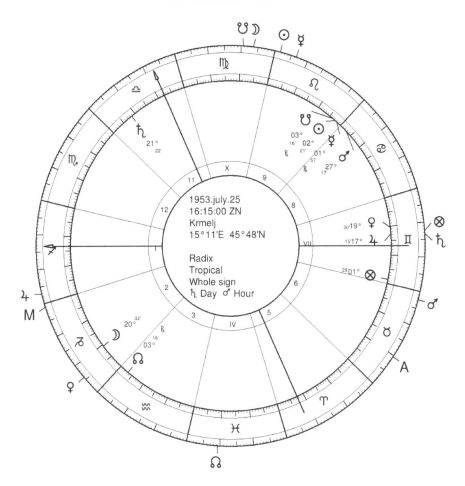

Gender: Male
Event: Birth of son
Date: 14th of August, 1979
Age: 26
Cycle ruler: Venus
Profection: Aquarius / 3th place
Ruler of the year: Saturn
Expected significators: Saturn, Venus, Jupiter, Lot of Sons, Lot of Children, 5th place, 11th place.

ANNUAL PROFECTIONS

The sign of annual profection is **Aquarius**, therefore **Saturn rules the year**. He is in the **11th place**, exalted and his ruler Venus is in the 7th **with Jupiter**. Furthermore, Saturn is conjunct Jupiter and Venus through his *dodekatemorion*. Additionally, he rules the **Lot of Sons** (18 degrees of Capricorn) and is co-present with the **Lot of Children 2** (9 degrees of Libra). This again brings us to Venus as the ruler of the latter lot and her conjunction with Jupiter, beautifully tying together the topics of children and relationships.

By profecting the cycle ruler Venus the profection is to Leo and thus Venus transmits to the Sun and to Mercury, who rules both her and Jupiter. If we profect the Sun, he transmits to Venus and Jupiter.

Profecting Saturn as the ruler of the year brings us to Sagittarius, thus again to Jupiter. According to Vettius Valens, when malefics transmit to benefics it signifies a more favorable year[14].

SOLAR RETURN

The ruler of the year **Saturn is in the 5th place** with the North Node, which could suggest child birth, but not without difficulties as Mercury, the ruler of the 5th is in the 12th from the 5th, retrograde and combust. Its conjunction with Jupiter who rules the 11th and the 8th again points to children, but also potential difficulties. Since Jupiter is advancing towards the IC a calamity is not to be expected. He has come under the Sun's beams, thus we again have an important planet being consumed by the Sun.

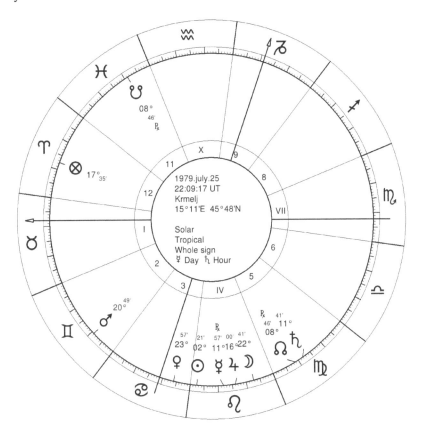

Venus, the cycle ruler is in Cancer, the 3rd place and strong at the IC, therefore the year is significant and busy. She rules the **Lot of Sons** which is **in the 1st place** at 3 degrees of Taurus. The Moon, her ruler and always an important factor is in the 4th place, **conjunct Jupiter.**

TIMING THE THEME IN THE SOLAR RETURN

In this Solar Return chart we can choose the significator among these candidates:

1. Saturn, who is the ruler of the year and is in the 5th
2. Jupiter, who rules the 11th and is with the Sun and the Moon
3. Mercury, who rules the 5th and is with the Sun and the Moon

Saturn is with the North Node in a night chart, thus very malefic. He possibly indicates a difficulty in relation to children, therefore he could signify a difficult labor or complications.

Jupiter is slightly under the Sun's beams, but rules the Ascendant in the natal chart and the 11th in the Solar return and is conjunct the 5th ruler Mercury.

Mercury is in the 12th from the 5th, under the beams of the Sun and retrograde, therefore we shall choose Jupiter as the most qualified of the three candidates.

The Moon is in the same sign as Jupiter, so the theme should unfold in the first month of the Native's year, thus between 25th of July and 25th of August.

MONTHLY PROFECTIONS

Going back to the natal chart, we start counting months from Aquarius, which is the sign of annual profection and remain in Aquarius, because we are looking at the first month as the possible time period. Saturn, the ruler of Aquarius and the North Node is exalted in the 11th and there is a trine aspect from Jupiter and Venus to Aquarius and to Saturn. The North Node signifies new, out of the norm and an increase. The native's son was born on the **14th of August.**

EXAMPLES 3 & 4

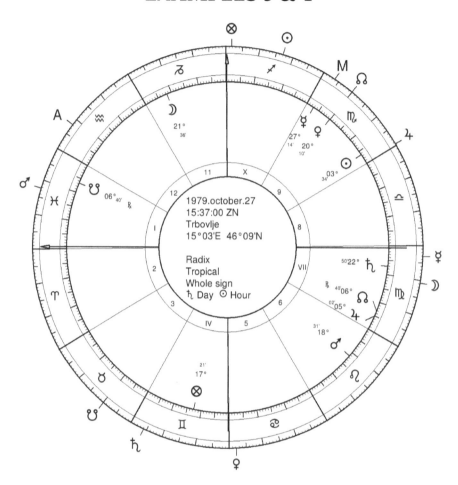

1979.october.27
15:37:00 ZN
Trbovlje
15°03'E 46°09'N

Radix
Tropical
Whole sign
♄ Day ☉ Hour

Gender: Female

Event: Birth of a daughter (1st child)

Date: 2th of February, 2013

Age: 33

Cycle ruler: Venus

Profection: Sagittarius / 10th place

Ruler of the year: Jupiter

Expected significators: Jupiter, Moon, Lot of Daughters, Lot of Children, 5th place, 11th place.

ANNUAL PROFECTIONS – 1ˢᵗ CHILD

The sign of the annual profection is **Sagittarius**, thus **Jupiter**, the ascendant ruler and significator of children is ruling the year. He is co-present with Saturn, the ruler of the 11ᵗʰ in the 7ᵗʰ place. Saturn also rules the Moon, the 5ᵗʰ ruler as the Moon is in Capricorn, the 11ᵗʰ place. Because this is a diurnal chart, Saturn behaves in a more tempered way and is partly auspicious due to ruling the fortunate 11ᵗʰ place and the Moon. He is also receiving the Moon in the 11ᵗʰ with a trine aspect and the Moon joins him with her *dodekatemorion*. **Saturn rules the Lot of Children 2** (23 degrees of Aquarius) which makes him very much involved with this topic. It is interesting to observe that the *dodekatemorion* of the Ascendant is conjunct the Lot of Children 2.

The **Lot of Children 1** at 17 degrees of Aries is not particularly involved. It is quite insignificant unless we profect the Sun. In this year he transmits to Mars in Leo, with Mars being in the 10ᵗʰ from the Sun, therefore Mars's rulership over this Lot is relevant when read within the context.

Another subtly involved Lot is the **Lot of Daughters** at 14 degrees of Gemini. Even if it isn't positioned in an important place or ruled by a time-lord it can still serve as an additional confirmation, because Gemini is the sign we get to if we profect the ruler of the year Jupiter. The Lot is also aspected by him.

SOLAR RETURN - 1ˢᵗ CHILD

The rising sign is the same as in the natal chart, therefore the year is of great importance. **The Moon, a significator of motherhood and the 5th ruler is rising in Pisces.**

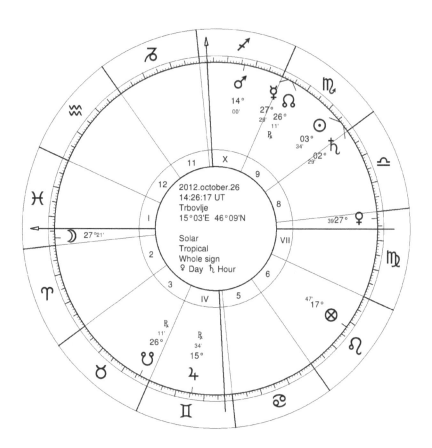

The 11th ruler Saturn is tightly conjunct the Sun, therefore he is in a deep combustion. The ruler of the year Jupiter is in the 4th place, retrograde and receiving the Moon by a square aspect. The Moon's placement alone could direct us to the theme of children, but the rest of the factors strengthen this further. The Moon carries an additional child-bearing power, because she rules the **Lot of Daughters** which is at 6 degrees of Cancer.

TIMING THE THEME IN THE SOLAR RETURN

In this Solar return we can choose the significator among these two candidates:

1. The Moon, who rules the 5th and is rising
2. Jupiter, who rules the 11th, the 5th by exaltation and is in the 4th

Since the Moon is ruled by Jupiter it is reasonable to profect her to the place of Jupiter, which is 4 signs away. This suggests the 4th month of the native's year which is from the 27th of January to 27th of February.

MONTHLY PROFECTIONS

Starting from Sagittarius which is the annual profection sign in the natal chart and counting 4 signs brings us to Pisces, the 1st place. Jupiter, the 1st lord is in the 7th with Saturn, who rules the 11th and the Moon (the 5th ruler). This is possibly as perfect as it can get. Her daughter was born on **the 2nd of February**, so the period suggested by our timing in the Solar return is confirmed.

Now, let's look at the birth of the 2nd child. This childbirth example is quite unique as it happened on the native's birthday and the child was born only one day after her Solar return, but she was already in hospital one day before.

Event: Birth of a son (2nd child)
Date: 27th of October, 2016 (at 16:01)
Age: 36
Cycle ruler: Sun
Profection: Pisces / 1st place
Ruler of the year: Jupiter
Expected significators: Jupiter, Moon, Lot of Sons, Lot of Children, 5th place, 11th place.

ANNUAL PROFECTIONS – 2nd CHILD

The ruler of the year is **Jupiter** who is in the 7th place with Saturn who rules the 11th place and the Moon, the 5th ruler. Again, we have a similar scenario, with Jupiter again ruling the year, so the same significations also apply in this case. Since it is a 1st place profection year, Jupiter transmits to himself. He is co-present with Saturn and Mercury's *dodekatemorion*. Saturn is, as we've seen a very important factor because he rules the 11th and the Moon. Mercury rules the **Lot of Sons** which is in Gemini. The cycle ruler is the Sun and Mercury is with him.

SOLAR RETURN – 2nd CHILD

The ruler of the year **Jupiter is strong at the MC**, conjunct the ruler of the Sun and the 5th place Mars. He is also conjunct Venus who rules the Moon. Their ruler Mercury is in Libra, the 11th place and thus in a mutual reception with Venus. This strongly ties together one's actions (10th place / MC) and the two places of children, 5th and 11th.

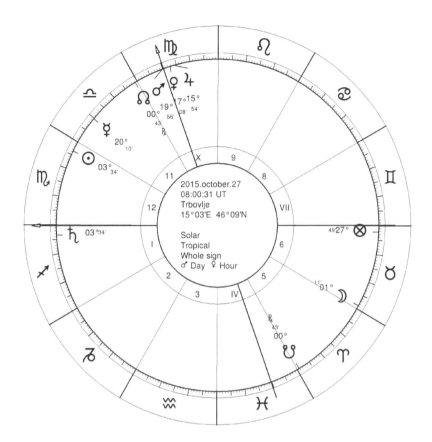

Saturn is about to rise and is under the rulership of Jupiter. Let's remember that Saturn is the 11th ruler in the natal chart where he is co-present with the ruler of the year Jupiter, therefore he gets activated and becomes significant. He also rules the 11th place in the Solar return by exaltation, and he also rules the **Lot of Sons** (15 degrees of Capricorn) which is aspected by Jupiter through an exact trine.

The Moon's placement is not very auspicious, but she is exalted and her ruler Venus is strong. Since we also have the themes of illness and hospitalization of the 12th place by Mars ruling both the 5th and the 12th, and the Moon is in the 6th, it would be appropriate to mention that the pregnancy had some complications with liver enzymes. Here Jupiter's conjunction with Mars might have played its part, because Jupiter rules the liver and the increased liver enzymes resulted in a large rash.

TIMING THE THEME IN THE SOLAR RETURN

In this Solar return chart we can choose the significator among these candidates:

1. Jupiter, who rules the year, the Solar return Ascendant and the natal Ascendant
2. Mars, who rules the 5th and is in an exact conjunction to the MC
3. Mercury, who is in the 11th and rules the 7th
4. Venus, the 11th ruler who is in a mutual reception with Mercury

As we can again see, there is a lot of focus on the 5th, 11th and 7th places. Jupiter is conjunct the 11th ruler Venus and 5th ruler Mars, therefore he is a great candidate. He is also in the 5th from the Moon and Fortune, which further strengthens his childbearing potential.

Mars as the 5th ruler, sitting right on the MC, is a strong candidate, too. Because this is a female native, we shall give preference to the 5th over the 11th as it is her that is bearing the fruit of her relationship with her spouse, the 11th from the 7th which is the 5th.

Mercury rules the other candidates and is in the 11th, but is in aversion to its domicile Virgo, which makes him questionable. It is important to note that his aversion to Venus is mitigated by their mutual reception.

Our last candidate Venus is strongly placed at the MC. She rules the 11th, is in mutual reception with Mercury and is conjunct Jupiter and the 5th ruler Mars.

At this point we shall choose between Virgo which holds three of our candidates and Aries which is the 5th place from the Ascendant and thus the place of children.

From the Moon to the Virgo stellium at the MC is five signs, therefore the theme would unfold in the native's 5th month which is from the 27th of February to 27th of March. From the Moon to Aries is twelve signs, thus the theme would unfold in the last month of the native's year which is between the 27th of September and 27th of October.

MONTHLY PROFECTIONS

Going back to the natal chart and counting 5 signs from Pisces which is the annual profection sign, we of course arrive to the 5th place and Cancer. Moon is in the 11th place, therefore the 5th month of the native's year seems to hold a great possibility for the theme to unfold.

Counting twelve signs from Pisces activates Aquarius, which itself is the 12th place, so at first glance we might prefer Cancer and the Moon as this configuration seems more straightforward. If we look a bit more carefully, Saturn, the ruler of Aquarius is in the 7th place with Jupiter and the North Node. He also rules the Moon in the 11th and receives her with a trine. There are more indications in this second set of symbols and as we have seen, the 12th place as the place of isolation, loss of life force, danger and hospitals has been very often involved in our case studies.

The native was hospitalized on the **26th of October**, just before her Solar return, one day before she gave birth to her son. It might be surprising that Mars was the important significator in the Solar return despite being the out-of-sect malefic. While he was ruling the 5th, he also modified the annual rulership of Jupiter to a slightly more malefic tone. Due to high liver enzymes the childbirth had to be triggered artificially and the amniotic sac had to be pierced with a spear-like instrument.

EXAMPLE 5

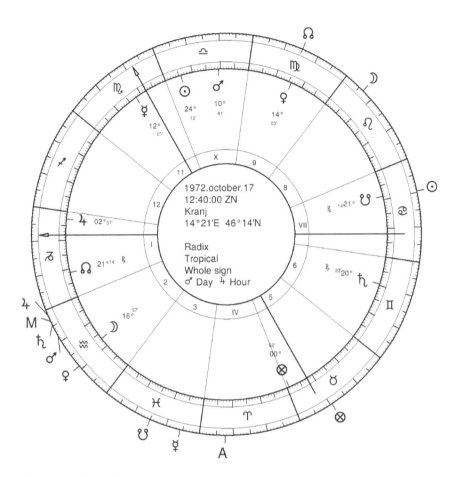

Gender: Female

Event: Birth of a daughter

Date: 4th of October, 1999

Age: 26

Cycle ruler: Venus

Profection: Pisces / 3rd place

Ruler of the year: Jupiter

Expected significators: Jupiter, Moon, Lot of Daughters, Lot of Children, 5th place, 11th place.

ANNUAL PROFECTIONS

At age 26 the annual profection was to **Pisces**, the 3rd place, therefore **Jupiter became the ruler of the year**. He is in the 1st place, co-present with the North Node. He is aspected by both the **5th** ruler Venus with a trine and by the **11th** ruler Mars with a square. Mars is also receiving Jupiter by exaltation.

The **Lot of Children 1** is at 25 degrees of Gemini, close to Saturn who rules Jupiter and the Ascendant. This Lot however is not the most productive one, since Saturn is in aversion to Jupiter, therefore we shall look at other children related Lots. The **Lot of Children 2** is at 5 degrees of Taurus, ruled by Venus who is trine to Jupiter. The **Lot of Daughters** is at 19 degrees of Virgo, near Venus, the 5th ruler. The importance of this Lot increases with the profection of the cycle ruler Venus, who transmits to Mercury (the Lot's ruler) in the 11th place. Additionally, the Sun transmits to Jupiter, therefore childbirth in this year is very possible, but let's look at what the Solar return chart has to say about it.

SOLAR RETURN

The ruler of the year **Jupiter is retrograde** in the 10th place in his domicile Pisces therefore we should pay attention to topics signified by Jupiter.

Venus who rules the cycle and the 5th place in both the radix and Solar return chart is in her domicile Libra, conjunct the Sun and therefore combust. The Sun rules the **Lot of Children 1** (4 degrees Leo) which adds to the importance of his conjunction with the 5th ruler Venus.

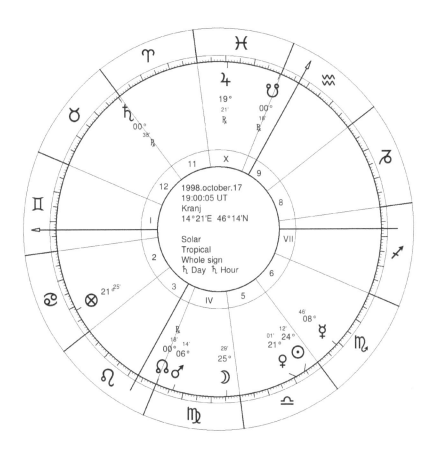

TIMING THE THEME IN THE SOLAR RETURN

In this Solar return we can choose between these candidates:

1. Jupiter who is retrograde and rules the year
2. The Sun-Venus conjunction in the 5th place

While the strongly placed and retrograde Jupiter is a natural candidate for the significator of the event, he doesn't rule any children-related places or Lots in this Solar return. On the other hand, the Sun and Venus are in the 5th place. Venus rules the 5th place in both the radix and Solar return chart, while the Sun rules the Lot of Children in the Solar return. The choice is obvious. The Moon transmits to Venus first in the second month of the native's year making this a very natural choice. The second time she transmits to Venus is when we profect her to Taurus, but this is the 12th place and we shall favor the 5th place instead. Our third option is her transmission to the Sun in Leo, the place of the Lot of Children. She profects to Leo in the 12th month. Let's go back to the radix chart and see which of the two months will be confirmed.

MONTHLY PROFECTIONS

In the radix chart we start the monthly profection from Pisces. In the second month the profection is to Aries, the 4th place. This is not very conductive to childbirth. The monthly profection in the 12th month is to Aquarius, the 2nd place, activating the Moon and four planets through their *dodekatemoria*. The selection is difficult, and in such cases it is of course important to use additional profections.

First, let's profect the Sun. We start from Saggitarius, because it is the 3rd place profection year. In the second month he profects to Capricorn, the 1st place. Capricorn holds Jupiter and the North Node which is an appropriate set of symbols, but Jupiter doesn't rule children-related places. In the 12th month the Sun profects to Scorpio, the 11th place where Mercury is located. Mercury rules the Lot of Children 1 and the Lot of Daughters which makes him strongly connected to the topic of children. Additionally, Mercury is configured to Jupiter and the 5th ruler Venus with a sextile. This makes the 12th month a better choice, but let's profect the Moon, too.

Starting in Aries, the Moon transmits to Venus in the second month when she profects to Taurus, and to Jupiter in the twelfth month when she profects to Pisces. In the twelfth month she arguably transmits more potently, because she transmits to Jupiter, Mercury (through its *dodekatemorion)* and also to Venus as the exaltation ruler of Pisces. The native gave birth to her daughter on the **4th of October, 1999**, thus **in the twelfth month**.

CHAPTER 7
ILLNESSES, ACCIDENTS & SURGERIES

1. Relevant places

As expected, it is the so-called evil places that are to be looked at when it comes to disturbances such as illnesses, accidents and surgeries. Out of the four difficult places (2nd, 6th, 8th and 12th) the 2nd place is the least frequently involved in these unfortunate events. The 12th place is significant, because it symbolizes isolation, hospitals, narcosis, coma and in general things that can terminate the bodily experience or existence. However, the two most important places for these topics are the 6th place where accidents and illnesses belong, and of course the infamous 8th place of surgeries, chronic illnesses, calamities and death.

2. Relevant planets

Besides malefic places it is natural to look at the two malefics, Mars and Saturn. The former symbolizing cuts, bruises, wounds, hits, breaks, needles, scalpels, blood and surgeons, while the later symbolizing diseases, obstacles, paralysis and death.

3. Relevant Lots

The **Lot of Fortune** is an important indicator of the body. If it is afflicted in some way, it can indicate difficulties pertaining to the body, provided there are also other indications present. There are however also specific Lots that symbolize illnesses and accidents more directly. In the examples we are going to use those I've seen effective in practice. These are:

1. **Lot of Calamity** – calculated by taking the distance from the in-sect malefic to the out-of-sect malefic, thus going from bad to worse. For day charts take the distance from Saturn to Mars, for night charts the opposite and add it or subtract it from the Ascendant.

2. **Lot of Illness** – I took inspiration for this Lot from the Lot of Marriage (Venus to the Dsc). We can create Lots connected to all the places, so in this case we measure the distance between Saturn (for disease) and the degree of the 6th equal house cusp (the same degree the Ascendant is at, but in the 6th whole sign place).

3. **Lot of Surgery** – the calculation is similar to the Lot of Illness, but here we measure the distance from Mars to the 8th equal house cusp.

4. A word of caution

Predicting this type of events is ethically questionable. I'm not in a position to judge whether an astrologer should or should not predict such events as it always depends on the circumstances and the moral judgment of the one who is performing the divination. Please, note that improper and untimely prediction of a calamity can have seriously negative consequences. The mind is a creative force as the Universe is mental. Seeding a negative event in one's mind has a great probability of the event actually manifesting.

5. Examples

EXAMPLE 1

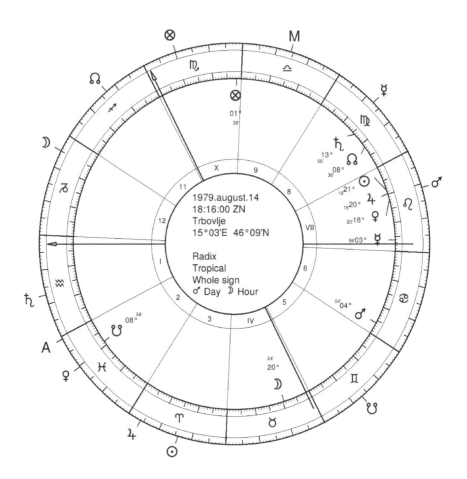

Event: Cardiac arrest
Date: 26th of March, 2007
Age: 27
Cycle ruler: Venus
Profection: Taurus / 4th place
Ruler of the year: Venus
Expected significators: Fortune, Mars, Saturn, Sun, Leo, Lot of Calamity, Lot of Illness, 6th place, 8th place.

In the early morning on the 26th of March 2007 the native felt a sudden attack of a sharp pain in the heart region. He was unable to breathe and he could observe his heart going wild and his chest thumping hard with an irregular rhythm. He was sure this was his end, but fortune was on his side and he survived. Before going to annual profections let us first look at the radix chart and the indications of health issues.

Saturn, the ascendant ruler is in the 8th place of death with the North Node, indicating possible sudden life-threatening events.

The ruler of Fortune is Mars, the out-of-sect malefic who is **debilitated in the 6th place** of illnesses and accidents. Mars is connected to stabbing, piercing, sharp pain and the sign of Cancer is associated with the chest, where the heart is. It is important to note that Mars's 12th part is conjunct the Sun which adds significantly to the possibility of difficulties with heart and spine. Furthermore, **Mars rules both the Lot of Calamity and the Lot of Illness** which are in Scorpio.

The Sun (the vital force) **is conjoined Mercury, the 8th ruler**, thus difficulties related to life force are clearly indicated.

Additional, but not so obvious indication of difficulties in this horoscope is **Jupiter**, because he rules the South Node (which is in Pisces) and is conjunct the Sun in Leo. Maybe the *cazimi* state of Jupiter can be interpreted very literally as being in **the heart** of the Sun. Therefore, in the context of vitality issues Jupiter is possibly a trouble-bringer, albeit a milder one due to simultaneously ruling the 11th house and his naturaly benefic nature. We can say that since he rules the South Node and the dark 2nd place he is a temporary malefic.

ANNUAL PROFECTIONS

Now that we've analized the malefic factors in this horoscope it's time to look at the profections. At age 27 the Ascendant profected to the 4th place, Taurus, transmitting to **Venus** who became the ruler of the year. This doesn't indicate a stressful event by itself. In fact, the native's year was overall quite pleasant.

Fortune, which we should look at for matters pertaining to the body has profected to the 1st place, Aquarius, **transmitting to malefic Saturn** who is in the **8th place**.

The Sun (the factor for vitality) and the cycle ruler Venus profected to the 10th place, Scorpio. They **transmitted to Mars who is debilitated in the 6th place and rules the Lots of Calamity and Illness.**

Vettius Valens says that when the Sun transmits to Mars it indicates a sickly and hazardous year[18]. Apart from this unfortunate event, the year was a busy one and there was a lot of progress (profections to angles) and fortunate events, indicated by the profected ascendant, involving the angular, exalted Moon and the angular albeit combust Venus.

So far, the natal chart and profections do hint at possible stressful events related to the body during this year.

SOLAR RETURN

The out-of-sect Mars, the 8th ruler, is very close to the Ascendant, conjoined the South Node who is weakening him, thus Mars can't create total harm.

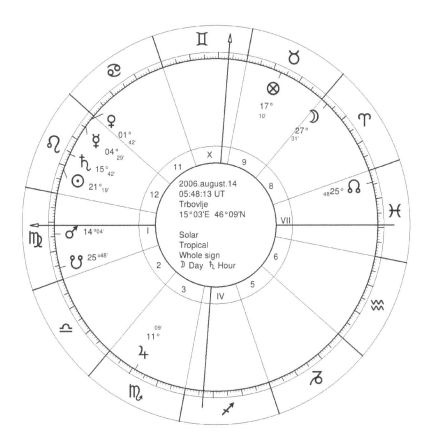

Mercury, the Ascendant ruler is in the 12th place conjunct the ruler of the year and Fortune ruler Venus. Two significators of body are together in the 12th place with a combust Saturn who rules the 6th place. Needles to say, this is inauspicious.

The Sun is in the 12th place conjunct Saturn, weak, but at least in his own sign. This alone already suggests that the native's health will suffer during this year.

The waning Moon is in the 8th place in Aries (12th place from Fortune), separating from the Sun, strengthening the 8th place theme. Jupiter is sextile to Mars and received by Mars, which mitigates the severity of the event.

SOLAR RETURN AS A SET OF TRANSITS

In order to find further confirmations for such a difficult theme, we shall now superimpose the Solar return onto the natal chart.

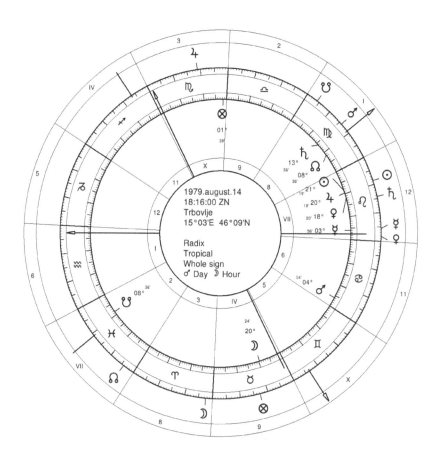

Saturn arrived to the position of Venus (ruler of the year and Fortune) in the sign of Leo which is the lower chest / Solar plexus area and is also associated with the heart organ. His conjunction to the radix Sun is of course of a great importance here as it can symbolize an extinguishing of the fixed fire of the Sun - the life force.

Mars, the profected ruler of the Sun arrived to the 8th place to the position of Saturn, the ascendant ruler who is with the North Node and thus amplified, indicating sudden traumatic events and possible near-death experiences.

Here we can again see how a Solar return chart superimposed onto the radix chart can bring additional clarity.

TIMING THE THEME IN THE SOLAR RETURN

In the Solar return chart we can choose the significator among these candidates:

1. Mars who rules the 8th place and is near the Ascendant
2. The 12th place stellium, because there are three important factors conjoined Saturn

If we leave the Moon in Aries, so that she transmits to Mars in the 1st place, then the period of the event is between the 14th of August and 14th of September. If we profect the Moon to Leo the event takes place between the 14th of December and 14th of January. By profecting the Moon to Virgo and Mars we get to the period one month later and by profecting her to the second of Mars's signs Scorpio we get to the period between the 14th of March and 14th of April. Now, this last option is a bit unusual, because Scorpio is housing Jupiter, who is in sextile with Mars and the Ascendant. This is where our prediction could turn out wrong, if we thought that the involvement of Jupiter should not be there. Let's not forget, that Jupiter can be considered as sort of a temporary malefic in the radix chart and that there had to be a benefic influence, too, because the native survived. So, to my (and probably your) great surprise it is the Moon's transmission to Jupiter and Mars in Scorpio that indicates the month of this unfortunate event (in which the native was actually quite fortunate) as the event took place on the **26th of March**, in the 8th month of the native's year.

MONTHLY PROFECTIONS

Let us see if the monthly profections in the radix chart confirm the period of the event we arrived to in the Solar return. If we start the profection from Taurus, which is the profection sign and move 8 signs we arrive at Saggitarius, therefore activating the unsuspected trouble-bringer Jupiter.

While we're not looking at transits, as this would clutter the book too much and because in classical astrology they are of a lesser importance, it is nonetheless appropriate to look at them, especially when in doubt about the outcome outlined by profections and the Solar return chart.

TRANSITS TO THE RADIX CHART

On the day of the event the retrograde Saturn's conjunction to Sun, Jupiter and Venus is immediately obvious. This in itself indicated difficulties, since three planets were in Saturn's clutches.

Upon further inspection Mars is transiting through the 1st place and is in opposition to transiting Saturn and radix Sun, Jupiter and Venus. The trio is being severely hammered. Additionally, a waning Moon was transiting over radix Mars that night. By looking at all these different charts we now have a quite clear idea that the native's body and life force were in serious danger.

EXAMPLES 2 & 3

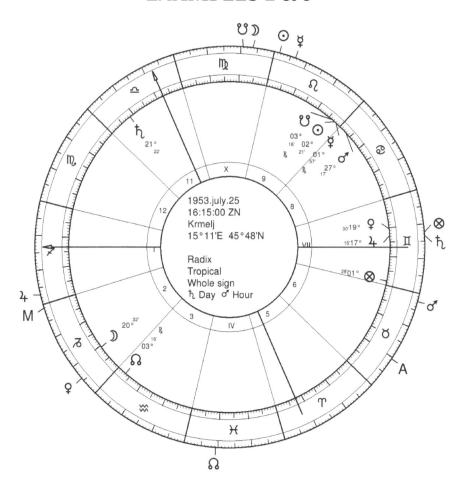

Event 1: Prostate cancer and surgery (1st surgery)

Date: 20th of November, 2013

Age: 60

Cycle ruler: Saturn

Profection: Sagittarius / 1st place

Ruler of the year: Jupiter

Expected significators: Fortune, Mars, Saturn, Moon, 6th place, 8th place, 12th place, Lot of Calamity, Lot of Illness, Lot of Surgery.

110

In this horoscope one can notice the **out-of-sect Mars, fallen and combust in the 8th place**. This is quite a strong indicator of illnesses that require surgery. Of course, Mars on his own is not sufficient to draw such a conclusion, but we can see that he is in opposition to the Moon, which is one of the indicators of the body. Furthermore, Mars is dominating Saturn, being in the 10th from Saturn, thus making the exalted and in-sect Saturn more maleficent that it appears at first. Saturn's *dodekatemorion* sits at the position of the Ascendant ruler Jupiter and is conjunct the *dodekatemorion* of Fortune, another indicator of the body. Additional testimony to physical difficulties is the conjunction of the Ascendant and Mars through their *dodekatemoria* in the 6th place of illness.

If we look at the relevant Lots, the **Lot of Illness is in the 8th place** with a fallen Mars. The Moon is opposing both, the Lot and Mars. Even more important in this case is the **Lot of Surgery** which is in Sagittarius, the 1st place. Jupiter is ruling the year and is conjunct Venus who rules the 6th place. Here we see a tremendous confluence of malefic factors which is bound to manifest at some time.

ANNUAL PROFECTIONS - 1st SURGERY

At the age of 60 the profection returned to the 1st place and the ruler of the year became Jupiter. He is in the 7th place, tightly configured to the angle and conjunct Venus. This seems auspicious at first glance, but we need to note that Venus is the out-of-sect benefic and she rules the unfortunate 6th place and the fortunate 11th place, thus giving mixed results.

SOLAR RETURN - 1ˢᵗ SURGERY

In the Solar return chart we have a repeating theme of an **out-of sect and fallen Mars,** but this time **in the 1ˢᵗ place,** conjunct the 12ᵗʰ ruler Mercury. Mars rules the **Lot of Calamity** which is at 11 degrees of Aries, right next to the MC, making ill health a prominent topic in this year.

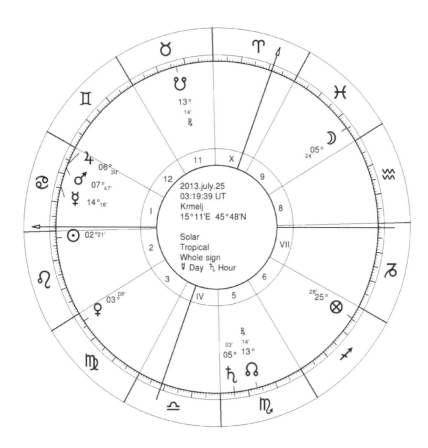

Of great importance is the exalted Jupiter, who rules Fortune and in the radix chart the Ascendant. Although Mars harms Jupiter to an extent it is the angular, diurnal and exalted position of Jupiter that prevents the year from having a disastrous outcome.

The Moon who rules the Ascendant is in Pisces, the 9th place, ruled by an exalted and angular Jupiter. She is **applying a trine aspect to Mars**, she is waning, but still full of light and **separating from Saturn**. Firmicus Maternus wrote:

> *"If the Moon, separating from Saturn, joins herself to Mars while full of light, she denotes illnesses and bodily defects,…" (Mathesis, book 4, chapter 3a, 4)*

As we can see, there are strong indicators of misfortune regarding matters of the body, but so far we haven't seen anything pointing to a surgery. If we look at Saturn again, he rules the 8th place, is conjoined the North Node in Scorpio, a sign ruled by Mars, symbolizing stings and cuts. Of course, as we've seen, his ruler Mars is in the 1st place, out-of-sect and fallen.

A more direct indication of a surgery is the **Lot of Surgery** at 19 degrees of Pisces, with its ruler Jupiter in the 1st place tightly conjunct Mars.

TIMING THE THEME IN THE SOLAR RETURN

Not all horoscopes speak with the same clarity and I'm not aware of a single technique that would work with consistent accuracy. In this example, the timing of the event to the month is not as precise as one would want it to be, but if the prediction was made, it would be only one month late, which for my standards is still great accuracy.

In this case it is natural to focus on the 1st place which holds important significators. Nevertheless, we have to carefully select between these:

1. Mars, because he repeats the radix theme and is with the ruler of the year Jupiter and the 12th ruler Mercury
2. Saturn, who rules the 8th place and aspects Mars and Jupiter.

For Mars we have three options: Aries, which is the 10th place and MC, Cancer and Scorpio. For Saturn we have Scorpio and Aquarius, which is the 8th place.

If we profect the Moon to Aries so that she transmits to Mars we get to the period between 25th of August and 25th of September. If we profect her to Cancer we get to the period between 25th of November and 25th of December. If we profect her to Scorpio and Saturn we get to the period between 25th of April to 25th of May. Lastly, if we profect her to Aquarius, the 8th place so that she again transmits to Saturn we get to the period between 25th of June to 25th of July.

MONTHLY PROFECTIONS

Looking back to the radix chart, the second month brings us to Capricorn, the 2nd place, which holds the Moon who rules the 8th place and Mars. The fifth month brings us to Aries and thus

Mars in the 8th place. The ninth month brings us to Leo, the 9th place and a dignified and joyful Sun, so this month is surely not one we'd connect with surgery. Lastly, the twelfth month brings us to Scorpio, the 12th place and thus again to Mars in the 8th. The choice here is a difficult one and an additional technique is required.

We can now try to dispel the mist by **profecting the Ascendant in the Solar return**. Out of the possible months indicated by the Moon's profection it is the 5th month that also stands out if we profect the Ascendant, because by doing so in the 5th month the Ascendant transmits to both Mars and Saturn in Scorpio.

In order to clarify it even more, we can also profect Fortune and it's with this step that the period of the event becomes clear. If we again look at the 5th month, Fortune profects to Aries, thus transmitting **to Mars** who is **in the 8th place from Fortune**. The 5th month of the native's year is the period between 25th of November and 25th of December. The surgery took place on 20th of November, thus 5 days ahead of the beginning of our selected period. In my practice I always allow a month of a leeway, because I've seen such minor discrepancies many times.

As is usual in the case of surgeries, the diagnosis comes first and the surgery is often performed months later unless it is urgent. In this example we've looked at the time of the surgery, but the diagnosis has been set in the native's previous year when the profection was to Scorpio, 12th place and the Ascendant was transmitting to the fallen, out-of-sect Mars in the 8th place. Additionally, the Sun was transmitting to Mars, who is in the 12th place from the Sun. As we saw in the previous example such a transmission was thought by Vettius Valens to bring a sickly and hazardous year. The disease itself manifested in a notable way in this exact year. It is important to note, that Mars here doesn't only indicate surgeries by symbolizing sharp objects, cutting, blood and surgeons, but that he also rules over the prostate gland. Let's now look at the Solar return chart for the native's previous year.

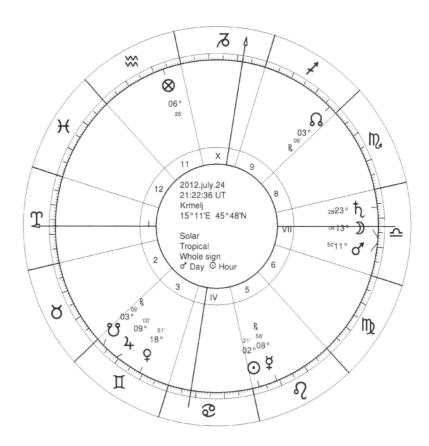

In this Solar return chart Aries is rising, thus Mars is prominent as the ruler of the year and the Solar return Ascendant ruler. He is in the 7th place, Libra, with Saturn. Mars also rules the difficult 8th place. The waning Moon is in between both malefics, which is very unfortunate when it comes to the health of the mind and the body. Indeed, the native went through a great turmoil in this year, both in terms health and marriage. Things could have been much worse without the intervention of Venus with her trine between the Moon and Saturn and her reception of the trio in Libra.

Taking the indications of the native's previous year into consideration many astrologers would predict ill health and possibly relationship issues for this year, which of course would be accurate. One could even predict a surgery, especially if the client would ask about it. Even if the prediction for the surgery was made, the only inaccuracy from the side of the astrologer would be the timing. However, at this point we need to remind ourselves, that an astrological consultation is not a hard-science, but a divination, thus a well attuned astrologer would most probably serve their client with correct answers and guidance.

Let us now look at the native's second surgery, which took place a few years later.

Event 2: Appendix removal (2nd surgery)

Date: 26th of January, 2017

Age: 63

Cycle ruler: Saturn

Profection: Pisces / 4th place

Ruler of the year: Jupiter

Expected significators: Fortune, Mars, Saturn, Moon, 6th place, 8th place, 12th place, Lot of Calamity, Lot of Illness, Lot of Surgery.

ANNUAL PROFECTIONS - 2nd SURGERY

The Ascendant has profected to Pisces, therefore Jupiter again became the ruler of the year. We have seen how Jupiter is involved in the native's distress in the initial examination of the radix chart.

The Sun profected to Scorpio, the 12th place, therefore transmitted to Mars, who is in the 8th and fallen. The Moon also transmitted to Mars as she profected to Aries. The cycle ruler Saturn transmitted to himself in Capricorn, but also to the Moon.

As we can see, the profections for this year are worse than in the year of the first surgery. While the first surgery was a distressful event, it went well and the native recuperated very quickly. This was not the case with the 2nd surgery, because unfortunately there were complications and just some days later the gall bladder and part of the small intestine had to be removed, too, because the intestines and the gall bladder got severely infected

118

and inflamed. The native survived the complications, but the improper actions of the doctor left him with chronic pain and the inability to function normally.

SOLAR RETURN - 2nd SURGERY

The Moon is rising in Aries and Mars is in the 8th place in Scorpio. This is of course quite illustrative of a surgery, even though Mars is in his domicile and in sect.

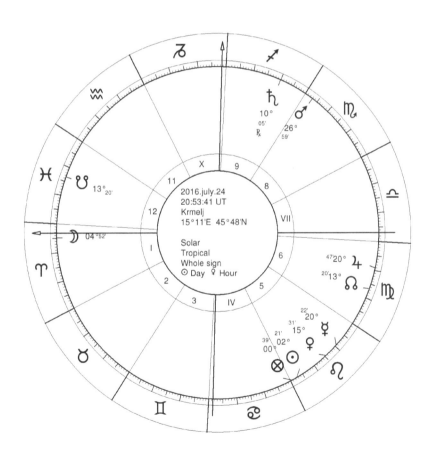

The ruler of the year and the radix Ascendant ruler **Jupiter** is in Virgo, **6ᵗʰ place** with the North Node. He also happens to be the ruler of the 12ᵗʰ place and the South Node. Additionally, he rules the retrograde Saturn who is in Sagittarius, dominating him through a square aspect. The domination of Jupiter over Saturn might be thought as a softening factor for Saturn, but let us inspect Jupiter more closely. He is out-of-sect, he rules the 12ᵗʰ place and the South Node (which takes away) and additionally he also rules the **Lot of Calamity** which is at 19 degrees of Pisces. Even more importantly, he rules the **Lot of Surgery** at 10 degrees Pisces.

TIMING THE THEME IN THE SOLAR RETURN

Here we have two obvious candidates for our significator:

1. Jupiter in the 6ᵗʰ place
2. Mars in the 8ᵗʰ place

The Moon transmits to Jupiter in the 6ᵗʰ month of the native's year, which is the period from 25ᵗʰ of December to 25ᵗʰ of January. Her transmission to Mars happens in the 8ᵗʰ month of the native's year, thus in the period from 25ᵗʰ of February to 25ᵗʰ of March. Since Jupiter is of great importance, because he is the ruler of the year, rules malefic factors and is sextile to Mars, we might choose him over Mars, but let's confirm this with the monthly profections in the radix chart.

MONTHLY PROFECTIONS

By starting at Pisces in the radix chart and counting 6 signs we get to Leo, which holds the Sun, Mercury and the South Node. This is not the confirmation we want. Counting 8 signs from Pisces brings us to Libra and Saturn, which is also not confirming the time period we've established in the Solar return. This is the first case in this book where the monthly profections and the timing method in the Solar return do not align perfectly. The monthly profections suggest the fifth month, because Mars in the 8th place is in the 5th sign from Pisces, the profection sign. In this case some flexibility is necessary and if the prediction for a surgery is made, it would be one or two months too early. For those seeking utmost precision, this might be insufficient, but I have to remind you, the reader, that the aim of this book is to present a methodology that is simple, based on whole sign houses and aspects and which can be easily practiced without a computer. It would be unrealistic to expected this set of techniques to yield results as accurate as more complicated, mathematical and astronomical techniques such as primary directions.

EXAMPLE 4

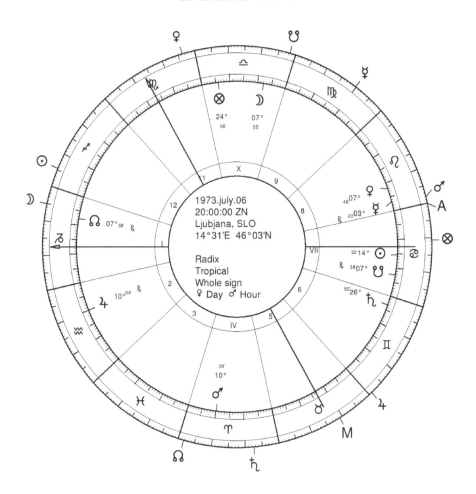

Event: Hospitalization due to SARS-CoV-2

Date: 16th of September, 2021

Age: 48

Cycle ruler: Mars

Profection: Capricorn / 1st place

Ruler of the year: Saturn

Expected significators: Fortune, Mars, Saturn, Lot of Calamity, Lot of Illness, Moon, 6th place, 8th place, 12th place.

ANNUAL PROFECTIONS

When the native was 48 years old the Ascendant has profected to its original position in Capricorn, thus Saturn was ruling the year. **Saturn is in the 6th place** of illnesses in the sign of Gemini which corresponds to the shoulders, arms and the upper chest / lungs in the human body, suggesting the native has to be careful about respiratory problems. Saturn also rules the **Lot of Illness** which is at 8 degrees of Capricorn, very close to the North Node, suggesting the native will come into the grip of illness very suddenly.

The cycle ruler Mars transmits to himself in Aries, but we should note that Aries also holds the *dodekatemoria* of Saturn and the North Node. Furthermore, Mars is out of sect, in opposition to the Moon and Fortune, and square to the Ascendant and the Sun. Additionally, Mars rules the **Lot of Calamity**, which is at 1 degree of Scorpio. With such a configuration health difficulties can be expected.

SOLAR RETURN

In the Solar return chart we have a repeating theme of **Saturn in the 6th place**. He is retrograde and in opposition to Mars and Fortune who are in the **12th place**. Fortune is in-between Mars and the ray of Saturn, which is detrimental, and this is especially so due to it occurring in the 12th place of hospitalization.

The Moon is in Gemini with the North Node, waning and with little light in the 12th place from the Sun, which represents a sudden threat to the native's vitality. This is especially so, because the Moon rules the Sun. It might be interesting to note that in India the North Node is often associated with viruses and bacteria.

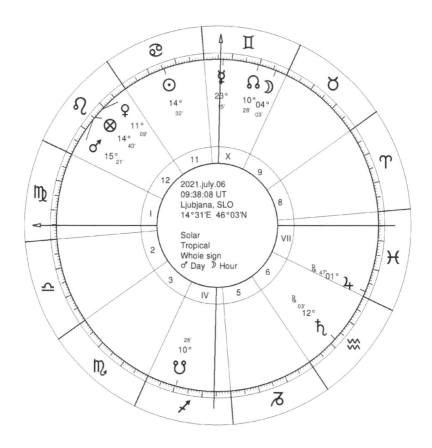

The Ascendant ruler Mercury is an interesting figure in this Solar return. He is strong - right on the MC and in his own domicile Gemini, indicating that the body is strong. On the other hand, **he rules the Lot of Calamity** which is at 8 degrees of Virgo, thus in the 1st place. Now we have a disease in the lungs (Gemini) which is very severe (Mercury at the MC). A friend asked me if the native will be able to overcome the seriously life-threatening condition he was in. When I looked at this Solar return chart it became clear to me that the body was strong enough to fight the infection, despite other factors pointing to a severe disease. The Sun (vitality) is advancing towards the MC and is in a favorable 11th place, therefore the life-force shouldn't be cut.

TIMING THE THEME IN THE SOLAR RETURN

Since the event in question is hospitalization it is natural to put our focus on the 12th place. The Moon transmits to Mars in the 12th place in the period between the 6th of September and the 6th of October.

MONTHLY PROFECTIONS

When we go back to the radix chart and perform monthly profections of the Ascendant this period, the third month of the native's year brings us to Pisces and thus to Jupiter. At first glance, this doesn't speak in favor of an unfortunate event, because we don't associate Jupiter with misfortune. However, Jupiter rules the 12th place, is retrograde and his ruler Saturn is in the 6th place. The *dodekatemorion* of Jupiter is in the 6th place with Saturn, thus Jupiter has quite a lot of connection to the two malefic places.

The third month of the native's year was indeed the time of the hospitalization.

EXAMPLE 5

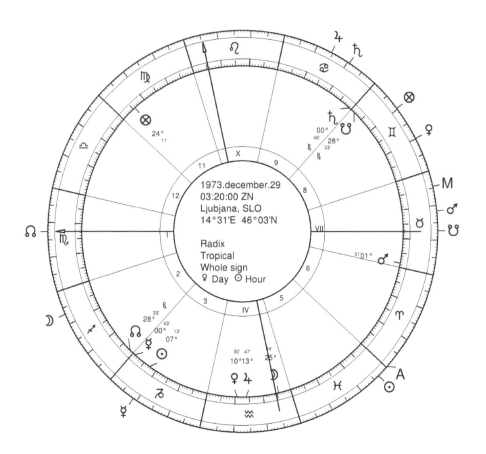

Event: Motorcycle accident and hospitalization

Date: 15th of August, 2016

Age: 42

Cycle ruler: The Sun

Profection: Taurus / 7th place

Ruler of the year: Venus / Mars

Expected significators: Fortune, Mars, Saturn, Lot of Calamity, Lot of Accident, the Moon, 6th place, 8th place, 12th place.

The native was a co-passenger on a motorcycle when a car hit them. Basically, her whole body was shattered (over 40 fractures), but the most injured part was her left leg. We see the Ascendant ruler Mars in the setting place, the 7th. He also rules the 6th place of illnesses and accidents and the *dodekatemorion* of the Ascendant is on the Pisces-Aries cusp. The out-of-sect Saturn, the ruler of both the Sun and the Moon, is retrograding into the 8th place of death, but is with the South Node, which takes away some of his maleficence. He is in a sextile to Mars, so the two malefics can bring difficulties without much action from the part of the native.

ANNUAL PROFECTIONS

The profection is to **Taurus, the 7th place**. The ruler of the year is **Venus**, who is well-placed, in-sect and conjunct Jupiter. The profection sign Taurus holds **Mars, who rules the Ascendant and the 6th place of accidents.** The Sun (the cycle ruler) is with Mercury, who rules the 8th place and is in an exact opposition with Saturn and in the 3rd place of short distance travel and transport. The Sun transmits to Saturn, which according to Valens, indicates a difficult year. Importantly, the Sun and Mercury are in a trine aspect with the 6th ruler Mars (the ruler of the year), which can hint a bit further at an accident that happens without the native taking a dangerous action as would be the case in a square aspect. Furthermore, the **Lot of Calamity** sits at 11 degrees of Capricorn. The 3rd place of this horoscope is connected to a lot of malefic factors. Luckily Fortune profects to Pisces and thus transmits to Jupiter. This is the native's saving grace. Jupiter and Venus are both overcoming Mars with a square, being in the 10th place from Mars, but their ruler Saturn is retrograding into the 8th place. Therefore, we can't be certain how serious the danger of an accident really is. Let's now take a look at the Solar return chart.

SOLAR RETURN

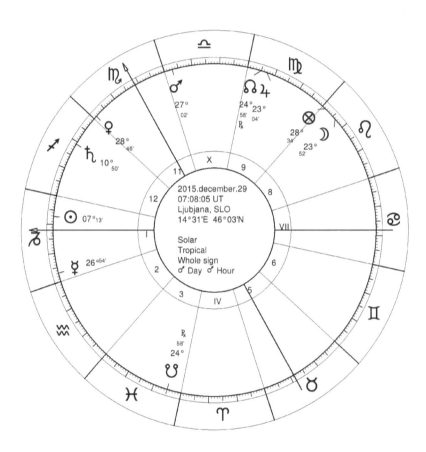

The Ascendant ruler Saturn is in the **12th place,** which is inauspicious and could indicate hospitalization. The Sun, who rules the **8th place,** and Mercury who, rules vehicles and the **6th place,** are in the 1st. The Moon and Fortune are in the **8th place.**

We can see that the body (the Ascendant, the Moon and Fortune) is linked with the three major difficult places, and at this point we can be certain that this is not a pleasant and healthy year. While the placement of Mars itself is not difficult, his maltreatment of Mercury through a square aspect is certainly fueling the 6th place theme we saw in the radix chart and is being repeated in the Solar return.

The **Lot of Accidents** is at 27 degrees of Leo, conjunct the Moon and Fortune. The Sun (its ruler) is rising in the 1st place. Many factors are pointing to an accident / injury or even death.

We should not neglect Venus who rules the year and is prominent along with Mars. She is placed in the fortunate 11th place, but sextile to the out-of-sect Mercury (rising after the Sun) who rules the 6th place. There is no doubt that the theme of friendship was prominent in this year, but the motorcycle trip with her friend unfortunately ended up tragically. It should be noted that Jupiter's reception of Saturn into Sagittarius, the 12th place and his aspect to Mercury is positive, because the native received proper medical care, which saved her life. This is, of course, in-line with the symbolism of Virgo.

TIMING THE THEME IN THE SOLAR RETURN

In this Solar return chart we have two obvious choices for the month of the event by profecting the Moon to:

1. The Sun as the ruler of Leo, the 8th place
2. The Sun and Mercury in the 1st place

Profection to Leo, of course, leaves us at the first month of the native's year. Her profection to the Sun and Mercury gets us to the sixth month. Let's go back to the radix chart and monthly profections to see if we can get some clarification about the month of the event.

MONTHLY PROFECTIONS

The first month seems suitable because we're in Taurus where Mars is, but the monthly transmission is to Venus, who is well placed and not connected to accidents. The sixth month is not a candidate because we get the transmission to Venus again. None of the months indicated by the profection of the Moon in the Solar return got confirmed by monthly profections. Here we need to further cross-reference the radix chart and the Solar return chart. In the radix chart, the sign that can most likely bring death or near-fatal events involving travel and vehicles is arguably Capricorn which holds the 8th ruler Mercury. This is the ninth month of the native's year, counting from Taurus. This also activates the perfect Mercury-Mars trine. In the ninth month of the Solar return chart the Moon transmits to Mars through Aries, which activates the Moon-Mars sextile. We are now very close, but one month late, because the accident didn't happen in the ninth month, but in the eighth month of the native's year, on the **15th of August, 2016**. While there is one month of discrepancy this is still a decent level of accuracy given the relative simplicity of the technique and a whole-sign approach. Of course, in real live readings of cases like this, the use of additional timing techniques would be necessary.

CHAPTER 8
MILESTONES & TURNING POINTS

The last chapter of examples is a relief from the previous dark one. Here we will look at milestones and turning points, the joyful and important events that leave a bright mark in our lives. Since the themes in this chapter vary greatly, the signifying planets and places will of course also vary.

1. Relevant Lots

Here we will focus more on specific topic-related Lots which are based on the distance between the relevant planet and the relevant equal-house cusp (the degree of the Ascendant in every whole-sign place, each 30 degrees apart). We will calculate them during the process of chart analysis, at the point when reaching for the Lot will be necessary.

2. Examples

EXAMPLE 1

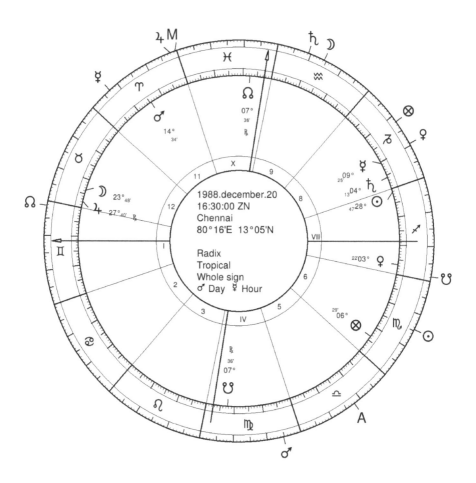

Event: Publishing of an astrological book

Date: 25th of March, 2021

Age: 32

Cycle ruler: Venus

Profection: Aquarius / 9th place

Ruler of the year: Saturn

Expected significators: Saturn, Mercury, 11th place, 10th place, 9th place, Lot of Writing.

ANNUAL PROFECTIONS

When the native was 32 years old, the Ascendant profected to **Aquarius, the 9th place**, therefore the ruler of the year became **Saturn**. The 9th place among many other things is connected to divination and astrology. The horoscope is diurnal, thus Saturn is the lesser malefic. It is interesting that in the Hellenistic tradition astrology was connected with Mercury and Saturn more so than with Jupiter as is the case in Indian astrology. After all, Saturn rules time and Mercury rules occult sciences. In this horoscope we have both of them conjunct in the 8th place which many would associate with occultism. **Mercury who rules the Gemini Ascendant** of course symbolizes writers and books. Saturn has his *dodekatemorion* in the 9th place, while that of Mercury is in the 11th in fiery Aries, suggesting a possible pioneering writing work.

The Sun transmits to himself in Leo and is with Venus in the 7th place of relations, suggesting the native will be well received and admired by other people. The same profection is of course true for Venus, the cycle ruler.

SOLAR RETURN

A very creative year is indicated by **the Moon as the 5th ruler rising in Pisces.** She is in the **11th place from Fortune**, which is favorable as it is the place of acquisitions and accomplishments. The Ascendant ruler Jupiter is exactly conjunct Saturn who rules the year. They are on the cusp between the auspicious 11th and inauspicious 12th place, therefore their agenda is uncertain at this point. Jupiter also rules the 10ᵗʰ place and the MC, therefore his conjunction with the 11ᵗʰ ruler is something we'd want to see if success was in question. The chart is diurnal, thus both of them are favorably disposed.

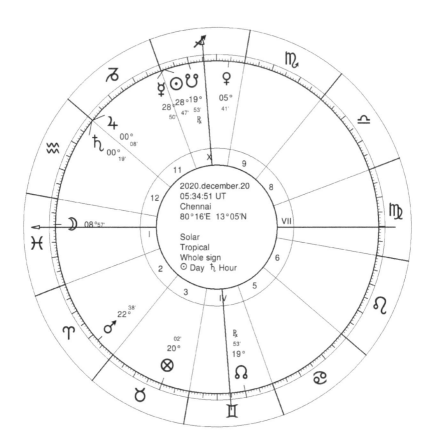

The Sun and Mercury are advancing towards the MC in the 10ᵗʰ place of career and actions. Let's not forget that Mercury rules the Ascendant in the radix chart. It is unfortunately not *cazimi* as it would appear based on the zodiacal longitude, because by declination it is not within 1 degree from the Sun, therefore it is combust, but this is another educating example regarding combustion in Solar returns.

The cycle ruler Venus is also in the 10th place but declining from the angle, therefore she is not a major factor. Nevertheless she shows that this is an important year for the native, because she is still in the 10th whole sign place. She also happens to rule Fortune in the 3rd place, which many astrologers would connect to writing, even though this is arguably a more modern association.

At this point, there is still something missing in order to conclude what exactly is going to happen. A book, writing and publishing is not very obvious, yet. The beauty of the Lots is in their immediacy. One can calculate a relevant Lot whenever there is a need for it. In this case I suggest taking the distance from Mercury to the 3rd equal house cusp. This will create a Lot that will focus on the Mercurial side of the 3rd place, thus writing, books and publishing. This **Lot of Writing** is at 12 degrees of Cancer and the Moon is at the Ascendant. Now it's becoming more clear that the 3rd and 9th places are giving the main flavor to this year.

At this point we might want to look back into the radix chart and find the Lot of Writing there. It sits at 18 degrees of Capricorn and at this point there is little doubt that the native writes books with an occult flavor and that something along these lines is about to manifest in this year.

TIMING THE THEME IN THE SOLAR RETURN

According to my judgment we have three candidates for the significator:

1. Mercury, who rules the radix Ascendant and is important in the annual profection. He is conjunct the Sun in the 10th place, advancing towards the MC
2. Venus, who rules Fortune and the 3rd place and is in the 10th place
3. Jupiter and Saturn conjunction, because it ties together the ruler of the year and the 10th ruler of the Solar return. The two are on the cusp between the 11th and the 12th places, therefore although they can help us in decoding the Solar return, they are not really the event bringers.

The most natural tendency here is to profect the Moon to Sagittarius, because it is the 10th place, the sign of the MC and houses Mercury, Sun and Venus. Furthermore, Jupiter also gets activated as the ruler of Sagittarius. It looks like the perfect scenario, but there is a small issue with Sagittarius. There is also the South Node in there, which is not something we'd want to see activated when someone makes an important new step in their life, a step into the unknown. For this reason we might opt for the activation of Mercury through Gemini instead. Although this is the 4th place it is nevertheless an angular place and it houses the North Node, thus Mercury gets activated as its ruler far more clearly than in activation through Sagittarius. Here we also have an interesting theme of bringing something innovative, written in the privacy of home, out to the public. By profecting the Moon to Gemini we get to the fourth month of the native's year, to the period between the 20th of March and 20th of April 2021.

MONTHLY PROFECTIONS

In the radix chart we start counting the months from Aquarius which is the annual profection sign. In the fourth month we arrive to Taurus where Jupiter and the Moon reside. Jupiter rules the MC and is in a trine with Saturn and Mercury. Even though Jupiter is in the 12th place, his activation as the MC ruler is still desirable. We should also note that there is a mutual reception between Jupiter and Venus. Additionally, Jupiter is conjunct the exalted Moon, therefore we should pay extra attention to Jupiter's placement.

The book was published on the **25th of March 2021,** thus in the fourth month of the native's year. He presented a fresh perspective and a different calculation of a classical medieval astrological technique.

EXAMPLE 2

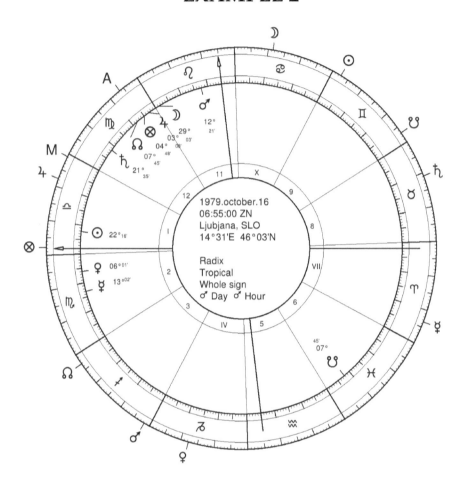

Event: Job contract

Date: 21st of February, 2022

Age: 42

Cycle ruler: The Sun

Profection: Aries / 7th place

Ruler of the year: Mars

Expected significators: Mars, Mercury, 11th place, 10th place, 7th place, Lot of Conctracts.

The native was very dissatisfied with his job which was causing him a lot of distress. He wanted to find a new job for a few years, but with no success. When I looked at his profections and Solar return I said to him that I'll be very surprised if he didn't get a new job in this year. It turned out that he indeed landed a great new job and was hugely relieved after months of extreme tension.

ANNUAL PROFECTIONS

The annual profection is to Aries, the **7th place of contracts. Mars is the ruler of the year** and is situated in the 11th place of gain and good spirit, advancing towards the MC. He is also co-present with the Moon, who rules the 10th place of actions and career.

If we profect the Sun who is the sect light and cycle ruler he also transmits to Mars, because the Sun is in the 1st place. As we saw earlier, such a transmission indicates a hazardous year. The native was in great distress and went through intense conflicts with authorities at his work. He was ready to take action, but the change presented a challenge for him due to the fixed sign of the MC and Mars.

SOLAR RETURN

In the Solar return we notice **Mars in the 11th place**, strongly advancing towards the MC and conjunct the Sun and Mercury. Mercury is right on the MC and rules the 10th and the 7th place.

139

The theme of the 7th ruler in the 11th and at the MC, conjunct the 10th ruler is repeated. Both Mars and Mercury are combust, which again confirms that in Solar returns this condition should be given great importance. Venus as the ruler of the 11th is receiving the trio from the 1st place. This ties the native very strongly to themes of work, actions in career and also contracts, due to involvement of Mercury, the 7th place and the sign Libra.

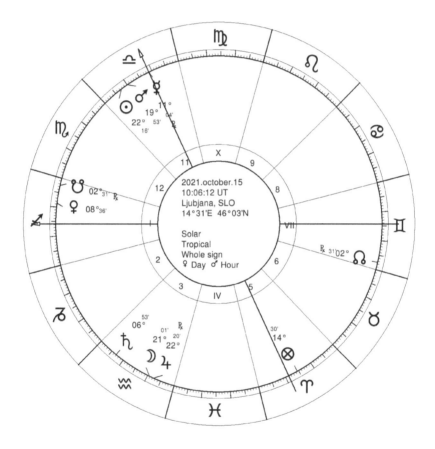

Since we are dealing with the question about possible new job contract we shall now construct the **Lot of Contracts**. We measure the distance from Mercury to the Descendant. The distance is 116 degrees and since we measure in a clockwise direction, we then subtract this distance from the Ascendant, which brings us to 11 degrees of Leo. The Sun in Libra now carries an additional signification of contracts, because it rules the Lot of Contracts.

TIMING THE THEME IN THE SOLAR RETURN

In this Solar return I would suggest choosing the significator among these candidates:

1. Mercury, who is at the MC and rules the 7th and the 10th place
2. Mars, who rules the year and repeats the radix theme
3. The Sun, who rules the Lot of Contracts

While both Mars and the Sun are good candidates they don't qualify nearly as much as Mercury does. Mars, apart from ruling the year and repeating the radix theme, doesn't rule relevant houses in the Solar return. The Sun, apart from ruling the Lot of Contracts also doesn't point towards a new job in any other way. Therefore, we shall select Mercury as the significator.

The first time the Moon transmits to Mercury is in the 5th month of the native's year when she profects to Gemini. The second time she makes the transmission to Mercury is in the 8th month when she profects to Virgo and the last time she makes the transmission is in the 9th month, when she transmits to the trio in Libra. All three transmissions are plausible, therefore we shall again confirm this with monthly profections in the radix chart.

MONTHLY PROFECTIONS

We start the monthly profections from Aries and in the 5th month we arrive to Leo, where we have the MC, Mars and the Moon. The monthly profection to Scorpio (2nd place) and Sagittarius (3rd place) is not as illustrative of a new job contract as Leo is, therefore we shall choose the 5th month of the native's year, the period between the 16th of February and 16th of March. He signed the new job contract and started his new job on the **21stof February**.

EXAMPLE 3

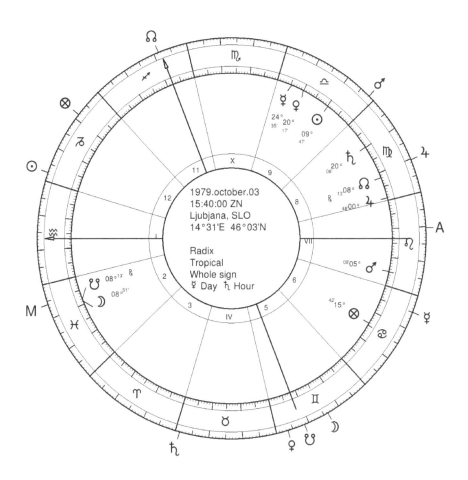

Event: Life-changing travel

Date: Mid-January, 2002

Age: 22

Cycle ruler: Venus

Profection: Sagittarius / 11th place

Ruler of the year: Jupiter

Expected significators: Jupiter, MC, 9th place, Lot of Travel

At age 22 the native went on an unexpected journey to a far away country, which turned out to be profoundly life-changing, because she found a new home there and didn't return.

ANNUAL PROFECTIONS

The sign of annual profection is Sagittarius, the **11th place** and the place where the MC is, therefore this might be a year of important actions. **Jupiter rules the year** and is situated in the difficult 8th place, co-present with the Ascendant ruler Saturn and the North Node. This is quite a vivid symbol of an unexpected journey to the unknown with many of the associated challenges. Indeed not everything was easy, but in the end she found her home and happiness there.

The 8th place is not the first place we'd associate with long-distance travel (this belongs to the 9th place). However, we can observe in practice that the places in aversion to the ascendant can also be connected with travel, because they take the native outside of the known, to places where life is quite different. This is especially true if one travels to a land with a culture that is very different and people are of a different race.

The **Lot of Travel** can help us see if the 8th place and Jupiter have something to do with travel. We measure the distance from the Moon to the 9th equal house cusp and then subtract the distance from the Ascendant, because we measure in a clockwise direction. We arrive at 24 degrees of Virgo, thus to the 8th place, not far away from Saturn (the Ascendant ruler). Therefore the 8th place carries the theme of long distance travels.

SOLAR RETURN

In the Solar return chart we see the ruler of the year **Jupiter exalted and rising**, co-present with the North Node, indicating expansion and bold action, because the Moon is in Aries, advancing towards the MC and is full of light. Jupiter rules the 9th place of long distance travel and is in a movable sign.

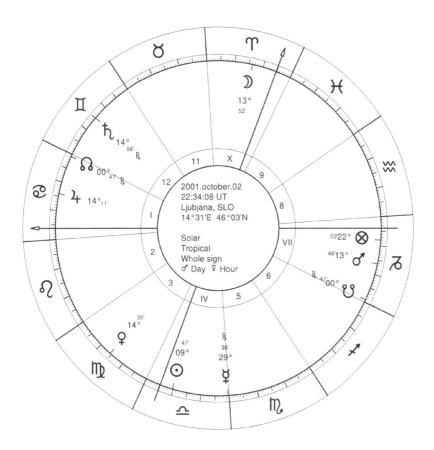

The Moon is dominating Jupiter by being in the 10th place from him and is receiving him in Cancer, empowering him with resources. Jupiter now expresses himself through the bold and adventurous actions of the Moon. Her ruler Mars, who rules the MC is exalted in the 7th place, is dominating the Moon and receiving her. Additionally he is in an opposition with Jupiter. To make the year even more important and busy, the Sun is in the 4th place in the movable air sign Libra, square to Jupiter and Mars and opposing the Moon. We have a lot of action indicated, due to the movable nature of the signs on the angles and planets residing in all angles. In modern terms, we have an angular and cardinal grand cross.

Since we have Jupiter as the 9th ruler rising, we shall look at the **Lot of Travels** in the Solar return, too. The distance from the Moon to the 9th equal house cusp is 17 degrees, therefore the Lot of Travels is at **9 degrees of Cancer**. This Lot gains an additional importance with the Sun's exact square to it.

TIMING THE THEME IN THE SOLAR RETURN

The candidate for the significator is quite obvious. It is Jupiter who rules the year and is associated with journeys.

The Moon transmits to Jupiter (and herself) in Cancer in the fourth month of the native's year, between the 3rd of January and 3rd of February.

MONTHLY PROFECTIONS

In the radix chart, we begin the monthly profection from Sagittarius and in the fourth month we arrive at Pisces, therefore

Jupiter is ruling the month. We also have the Moon placed therein, thus what we have seen in the Solar return gets confirmed nicely. Indeed, the native embarked on this life-changing journey in **mid-January 2002**.

EXAMPLE 4

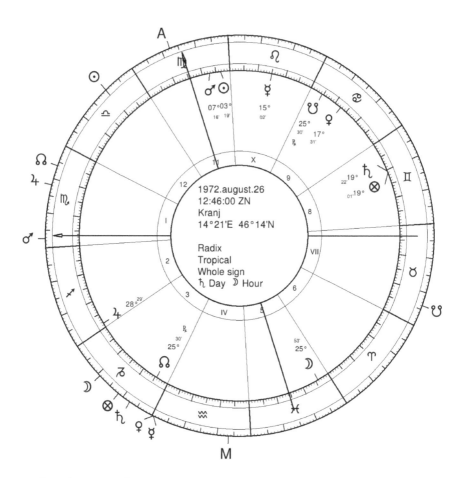

1972.august.26
12:46:00 ZN
Kranj
14°21'E 46°14'N

Radix
Tropical
Whole sign
♄ Day ☽ Hour

Gender: Female

Event: Life-changing business travel

Date: 4th of October, 2017

Age: 45

Cycle ruler: The Sun

Profection: Leo / 10th place

Ruler of the year: The Sun

Expected significators: Jupiter, 9th place, Lot of Travel, MC, 10th place.

On the 4th of October, 2017 the native went on a business trip to a faraway country. She was invited there by a new friend. At that time she was seeking a way to make a breakthrough as a life/business coach and this was her opportunity to plug into a vast business network. Soon afterwards, while staying in this foreign country, she fell in love with the man who had invited her over and a few months later they got married. This is an example that would fit in chapter 5, but since this was a year of two major turning points in her life I have decided to include it in this chapter.

ANNUAL PROFECTIONS

At age 45 the profection was to **Leo, 10th place**, therefore the Sun became the ruler of the year. He is in the 11th place, conjunct Mars who rules the Ascendant. They are past the MC, but still quite close. It is important to be aware of the **mutual reception** between the Sun and Mercury, happening in the **10th and 11th places**. It is clear that this is a year of major actions related to career, success and material gain.

The Sun as the cycle and year ruler transmits to Saturn in the 8th place and arguably to Mercury as the ruler of Gemini, who is in the 10th. Saturn is in the 10th place from the Sun indicating slow developments in career, but also lasting results. The year was of course full of challenges, needs for adjustment and the overcoming of her fears.

Both the Moon and Fortune profect to places ruled by Jupiter (Sagittarius and Pisces). Jupiter is in the 2nd place in his domicile, square to both luminaries. Finances and career are the main focus of the year without a shadow of a doubt.

SOLAR RETURN

Jupiter is rising in Libra and is received by Venus, who is at the MC. In the context of the picture painted by annual profections with the emphasis on the 10th and 11th places this should be a year of expansion, growth and happiness, even if the Sun as the ruler of the year is in the 12th place.

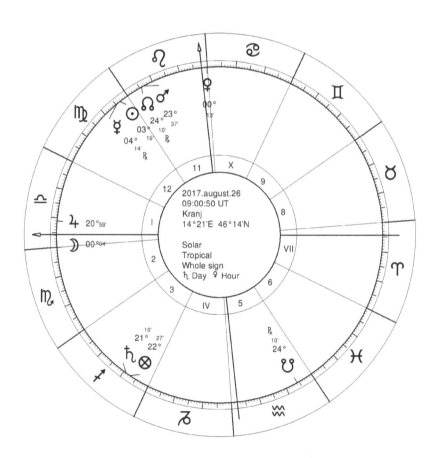

It is interesting to note that the Sun is conjunct an exalted Mercury who is in turn combust and retrograde. Mercury rules the 9th place of travels. We can again see the involvement of a dark place (12th) and two travel significators (Jupiter in the 1st and as the 9th ruler with the Sun in the 12th). Additionally, Mercury rules the **Lot of Travel**, which we construct by taking the distance from the Moon to the 9th equal house cusp. The Lot is at 20 degrees of Gemini.

An interesting feature of this Solar return is one that we have seen before. The Ascendant ruler Venus and the Descendant ruler Mars, male and female are co-present in Leo, 11th place (the place where the MC is). Mars is conjunct the North Node, thus symbolizing both a new man and an ambitious step into the unknown.

Since we have two themes unfolding, let us check how strongly the marriage theme is indicated, first by calculating the **Lot of Marriage** (the distance from Venus to Saturn for a female). It is at 16 degrees of Pisces, therefore ruled by Jupiter who is rising in Libra and his ruler is at the MC. The **Lot of Union** (from Venus to the Descendant) is at 21 degrees of Cancer, 10th place and its ruler the Moon is about to rise. The **Lot of Husband** is at 15 degrees of Libra, thus in the 1st place and its ruler Venus is at the MC. The native was reluctant to marry and was torn between two options. One was leaving the worldly ambitions and living an ashram life instead (Venus with the South Node in the 9th place). The second one was to get married and pursue success as a coach. When I saw her Solar return chart I said to her that I'm looking forward to being invited to a wedding. She was in a disbelief. Some months later she sent me her wedding photo.

TIMING THE THEME IN THE SOLAR RETURN

These are our options for choosing the significator:

1. Jupiter who is rising
2. Sun-Mercury conjunction

Jupiter is a strong candidate, because he symbolizes travel and is in a movable sign Libra, which is a symbol of trade, business and relationships. The first time the Moon transmits to Jupiter is in the 2nd month of the native's years, when she profects to Sagittarius, the 3rd place, which houses the 4th ruler Saturn. He is in the 12th from the 4th, thus taking the native away from home. Jupiter and Saturn are in a tight sextile and Jupiter is receiving Saturn.

The Sun-Mercury conjunction is also an appropriate choice, because we have the MC ruler and the 9th ruler conjunct. The Moon transmits to them in the eleventh month.

MONTHLY PROFECTIONS

In the radix chart the monthly profection in the second month is to Virgo, the 11th place, with the Sun, Mars and the MC therein. In the 11th month the profection is to Gemini, the 8th place, which doesn't speak as clearly about taking an ambitious action as the profection to Virgo, because Virgo triggers the Sun-Mercury mutual reception.

The native went on this life changing business travel on the **4**[th] **of October**, 2017, which is the second month, as suggested by the profection to Virgo in the radix chart, and profection of the Moon to Sagittarius in the Solar return.

EXAMPLE 5

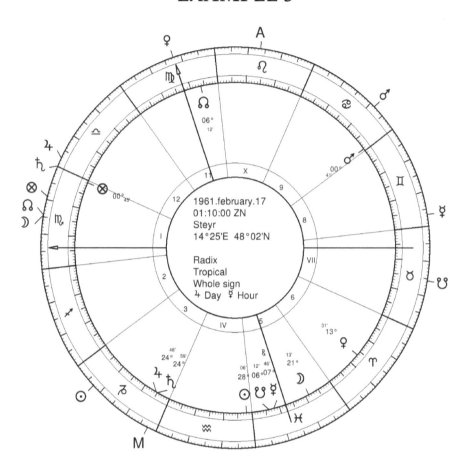

1961.february.17
01:10:00 ZN
Steyr
14°25'E 48°02'N

Radix
Tropical
Whole sign
♃ Day ☿ Hour

Gender: Male

Event: Music work abroad

Date: 1st of October, 1989

Age: 28

Cycle ruler: Venus

Profection: Pisces / 5th place

Ruler of the year: Jupiter

Expected significators: Jupiter, 9th place, Lot of Travel, MC, 10th place.

The native signed a music contract in a foreign land on the 1ˢᵗ of October 1989. Since then he has worked in this foreign country for many years, returning to his homeland only to visit.

ANNUAL PROFECTIONS

The sign of the annual profection is **Pisces, the 5ᵗʰ place**, therefore **Jupiter rules the year**. He is conjunct Saturn in Capricorn, the 3ʳᵈ place of short distance travels. Since the foreign country he worked in is the neighboring country, we can consider this to be a short distance travel, but since the native's work also involved wider traveling we shall also pay attention to long-distance travel factors. Pisces also holds the Moon, who rules the **9ᵗʰ place** of long distance travel and foreign places and Mercury who rules **the MC**. The 5ᵗʰ place is the place of creative expression and both the Moon and Mercury are connected with music – Mercury for skills with instruments and the Moon for rhythm and melody.

If we profect the Moon she moves to Cancer, the **9ᵗʰ place** and transmits to Mars, the Ascendant ruler. This connects the native with travel in a very direct way. If we profect the Sun, he transmits to Mercury. The cycle ruler Venus transmits to the Sun, the 10ᵗʰ ruler. At this point travel and creative work seem to be the main themes of this year.

To get an additional testimony for travel, we shall look at the **Lot of Travel** (Moon to the 9ᵗʰ equal cusp). The Lot is at 27 degrees of Pisces. Let us now look at what the Solar return chart will reveal.

SOLAR RETURN

The ruler of the year **Jupiter is in the 9th place**. The 9th ruler and the cycle ruler Venus is with the Sun, combust in the 6th place of work. She is co-present with Mercury who rules the Ascendant, the 10th place and the MC. Additionally, the Sun rules the Lot of Travel (14 degrees of Leo). The themes of travel and work are tied up beautifully also in the Solar return chart.

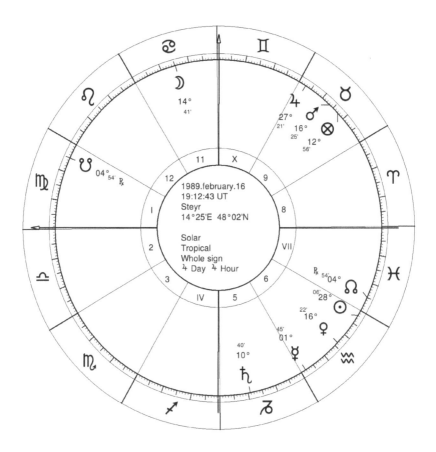

The Moon is in the auspicious 11th place in her domicile, advancing towards the MC. Since the native's work revolved around music we shall see if the **Lot of Music** is in some way activated. We measure the distance from the Moon (music) to the 5th equal house cusp (creative expression) and count this distance from the Ascendant in a clockwise direction, because the shorter distance between the Moon and the 5th cusp is clockwise. We arrive at 14 degrees of Aries, therefore Mars rules music in this chart. He is with Jupiter and Fortune in the 9th place, carrying musical expression into the foreign land. Additionally the 9th place is Taurus which is the Moon's exaltation. It is in this Venus-ruled fixed earth sign that beautiful forms take place.

TIMING THE THEME IN THE SOLAR RETURN

I think most astrologers would agree that the best options for selecting the months would be:

1. Jupiter and Mars in Taurus
2. Sun-Venus-Mercury in Aquarius

The Moon transmits to Jupiter and Mars in the eleventh month of the native's year and to the Sun-Venus-Mercury trio in the eighth month.

MONTHLY PROFECTIONS

Going back to the radix chart, we count the months from Pisces. The fifth month brings us to Libra and Venus. Venus is in the 6th place of work and has her *dodekatemorion* at the MC.

The eleventh month brings us to Capricorn and thus to Saturn and Jupiter. Both of these places are in agreement to what we've seen in the Solar return, therefore we need to pay closer attention. Libra also holds the *dodekatemoria* of Saturn and Jupiter, therefore we shall choose Libra and the eighth month of the native's year, which is between the 17th of September and 17th of October. The native started with his music work in a foreign land on the **1st of October**.

A NOTE ON COMBUSTION AND RETROGRADE PHASE

As we could see, many of the Solar returns (13 out of 20) had an important planet combust or retrograde. This has profoundly challenged my views on these two concepts and I have thought about it in philosophical terms. Since we're looking at a Solar return chart which is based on the Sun's annual return, a combustion might even be desirable, provided it happens in a favorable place. In combustion the Sun (consciousness) consumes that which is represented by the planet that is consumed by the Sun's light, therefore the manifestation of that planet comes into the awareness of the native. A retrograde planet moves contrary to the norm, is closer to the Earth and therefore draws attention to itself - something out of the ordinary is happening.

CHAPTER 9
ADDITIONAL TIME-LORDS

Now that we have analyzed events through profections and Solar returns, which for the most part were sufficient to get a rather clear picture of what the year would bring, we can incorporate additional time-lord techniques in order to achieve greater accuracy. A quite popular technique is the activation of planets at the completion of their minor years, or their halves or thirds. This is a traditional technique first found in the text of Vettius Valens, but in practice I haven't found it to be reliable enough, unless we give it a few years of leeway. Plus, the halves and thirds of their years give us too many options. There are of course other time-lord techniques, but apart from the medieval Firdaria, which is based on the synodic cycles of planets and therefore has the Sun as its basis, I haven't come across one that conceptually fits profections and Solar returns. Since Firdaria is well known and a wonderful book has already been written on it by Aswin Subramanyan[19], I have decided to instead present a time-lord technique I have developed myself, inspired by the sign based timing techniques of Jaimini's system of Indian astrology[20] and the Hellenistic principle of sect. The technique is simple and does not require a lot of computation. It is very individualized and because I have found it useful, I'm now sharing it in this book.

1. 1. Trails of the Stars

In the second chapter I introduced the concept of a 12-year cycle ruler, since every 12 years the profection cycle repeats and the same sign is activated. While the cycle repeats, our life experiences are not the same every 12 years. They might share a common theme, but the outcomes can be drastically different. Besides looking at the cycle ruler in order to understand what the difference will be, we can of course use Solar return charts which are the main focus of this book. Solar returns are, however, not very practical as a snapshot technique, because if we want to predict quickly, we can't get a fast impression of the difference because we need to look at a Solar return chart for every year, which is time-consuming. It was for this reason that I began to search for time-lord techniques built on the fundamental principle of profections (1 sign = 1 year), which could enable me to see the difference between 12-year cycles without having to look at many Solar return charts at once. Usually primary directions of the Ascendant through the bounds are performed for this purpose, but this technique is built on the principle of diurnal rotation and an approximately 1 degree = 1 year principle. I am not saying that directions are not useful alongside profections, but I've been searching for something that is conceptually more in line with annual revolutions. Since I could not find such a time-lord technique I began to experiment. I found the basic inspiration for the technique I'm about to describe in the enigmatic system of Jaimini from India, where various *daśās* (Indian equivalent to time-lords) are all based on the principle of 1 sign = 1 year. Those are all sign-based *daśās*, with a sign being assigned a span of various years. In my method I wanted to assign years to

162

planets instead of signs, but based on the principle of sign distances. The method will be explained after we determine the luminary from which the rulership of time will begin.

1. 2. The initiator

Ancient techniques for calculating the length of life require that we select the e*pikratétor* or the predominator of the horoscope. This is usually the Sun by day or the Moon by night, provided they meet certain criteria. If they don't, then the other luminary takes the place of the predominator, or sometimes even Fortune or the Ascendant. Since the selection of the predominator is not a part of this technique we will not examine it. The Trails of the Stars time-lord technique does require a similar selection of the luminary from which we start the releasing or counting of time, but the rules are a bit simpler than those for selecting the predominator and are based on whole-sign places. We shall call the luminary that begins the counting of years **the initiator**.

The initiator can only be one of the two luminaries. In a diurnal horoscope the initiator is the Sun, unless he is in the 8th or the 12th place (with the 8th place having some exceptions). In such a case the Moon replaces the Sun, provided she is not in the 12th or the 6th place. The same rules apply for a nocturnal horoscope, where the Moon is the initiator, unless she is in the above mentioned places. If both luminaries are in difficult places, then we select the one that is in the 8th or the 2nd, since these two places are succeedent and will eventually move to an angle. In order to not leave too much space for speculation I've decided to write down all the possible scenarios where the luminary of the sect is replaced by the other.

BY DAY (places in order of diurnal rotation):

The Sun in the 12th, the Moon in the 1st = the Moon

The Sun in the 12th, the Moon in the 12th = the Sun

The Sun in the 12th, the Moon in the 11th = the Moon

The Sun in the 12th, the Moon in the 10th = the Moon

The Sun in the 12th, the Moon in the 9th = the Moon

The Sun in the 12th, the Moon in the 8th = the Moon

The Sun in the 12th, the Moon in the 7th = the Moon

The Sun in the 12th, the Moon in the 6th = the Sun

The Sun in the 12th, the Moon in the 5th = the Moon

The Sun in the 12th, the Moon in the 4th = the Moon

The Sun in the 12th, the Moon in the 3rd = the Moon

The Sun in the 12th, the Moon in the 2nd = the Moon

The Sun in the 8th, the Moon in the 1st = the Moon

The Sun in the 8th, the Moon in the 12th = the Sun

The Sun in the 8th, the Moon in the 11th = the Moon

The Sun in the 8th, the Moon in the 10th = the Moon

The Sun in the 8th, the Moon in the 9th = the Moon

The Sun in the 8th, the Moon in the 8th = the Sun

The Sun in the 8th, the Moon in the 7th = the Moon

The Sun in the 8th, the Moon in the 6th = the Sun

The Sun in the 8th, the Moon in the 5th = the Moon

The Sun in the 8th, the Moon in the 4th = the Moon

The Sun in the 8th, the Moon in the 3rd = the Moon

The Sun in the 8th, the Moon in the 2nd = the Sun

Note: The Sun in the 6th and 2nd places will always be below the horizon, but if he is up to 6 degrees below the horizon the horoscope is considered to be diurnal.

The Sun in the 6th, the Moon in the 1st = the Moon
The Sun in the 6th, the Moon in the 12th = the Moon
The Sun in the 6th, the Moon in the 11th = the Moon
The Sun in the 6th, the Moon in the 10th = the Moon
The Sun in the 6th, the Moon in the 9th = the Moon
The Sun in the 6th, the Moon in the 8th = the Moon
The Sun in the 6th, the Moon in the 7th = the Moon
The Sun in the 6th, the Moon in the 6th = the Sun
The Sun in the 6th, the Moon in the 5th = the Moon
The Sun in the 6th, the Moon in the 4th = the Moon
The Sun in the 6th, the Moon in the 3rd = the Moon
The Sun in the 6th, the Moon in the 2nd = the Moon

If the Sun is in the 9th place and the Moon is in the 1st or the 7th place and **above the horizon**, then the Moon replaces the Sun. Since the 9th place is the place of the Sun's joy, the Moon must be above the horizon in order to be able to take the Sun's role as the initiator. She can replace the Sun also if she is in the 11th or the 10th place.

BY NIGHT (places in order of diurnal rotation):

The Moon in the 12th, the Sun in the 6th = the Moon
The Moon in the 12th, the Sun in the 5th = the Sun
The Moon in the 12th, the Sun in the 4th = the Sun
The Moon in the 12th, the Sun in the 3rd = the Sun
The Moon in the 12th, the Sun in the 2rd = the Sun

The Moon in the 8th, the Sun in the 6th = the Moon

The Moon in the 8th, the Sun in the 5th = the Sun

The Moon in the 8th, the Sun in the 4th = the Sun

The Moon in the 8th, the Sun in the 3rd = the Sun

The Moon in the 8th, the Sun in the 2rd = the Moon

The Moon in the 6th, the Sun in the 6th = the Moon

The Moon in the 6th, the Sun in the 5th = the Sun

The Moon in the 6th, the Sun in the 4th = the Sun

The Moon in the 6th, the Sun in the 3rd = the Sun

The Moon in the 6th, the Sun in the 2rd = the Sun

The Moon in the 2nd, the Sun in the 6th = the Moon

The Moon in the 2nd the Sun in the 5th = the Sun

The Moon in the 2nd, the Sun in the 4th = the Sun

The Moon in the 2nd, the Sun in the 3rd = the Sun

The Moon in the 2nd, the Sun in the 2rd = the Moon

If the Moon is in the 3rd place of her joy, she can be replaced by the Sun only if he is in the 1st or the 7th place and also if he is in the 5th or the 4th place.

Perhaps these rules should be refined with time as more and more horoscopes will be examined with the technique, but since they have proven to be quite adequate in my tests, let them serve as a guideline for now.

1. 3. The technique explained

We know that each planet has its male or diurnal and female or nocturnal domicile. The Sun and the Moon only have one domicile each (Leo and Cancer). This division of diurnal and nocturnal domiciles is well known and commonly accepted, but we unfortunately rarely see it put in use. Our technique here will, like most Hellenistic or traditional techniques comply with the principle of sect and also take diurnal and nocturnal domiciles into the account. The procedure is as follows:

1. We determine the initiator (as described earlier).

2. We count how many signs the initiator has traveled from its domicile. If in domicile, it gets 12 years. If in the 2nd sign from it, it gets 1 year. If in the 12th sign from it, it gets 11 years, etc.

3. We continue in the ascending order by speed, so if we started with the Sun, the next time-lord will be Mars and if we started with the Moon, the next time-lord will be Mercury. We count the signs according to the sect, thus by day from the diurnal domicile and by night from the nocturnal one.

4. When the full cycle of time-lords is complete, the rulership of time is handed over to the sect Light again.

I named this technique Trails of the stars, because the planets are leaving a trail from their domicile that represents years they have traversed, thus the amount of years they rule. To demonstrate this time-lord technique I will use a few of the horoscopes from earlier chapters. We will now look at how this time-lord technique can help to direct our focus.

2. 1. Examples

EXAMPLE 1

(from chapter 5, example 4)

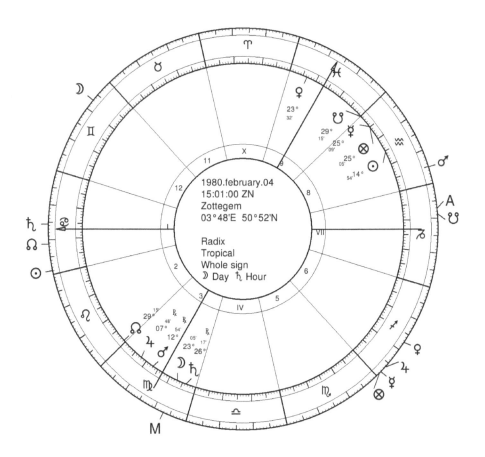

Event: Wedding

Date: 12th of October, 2019

Age: 39

Cycle ruler: The Sun

Profection: Libra / 4th place

Ruler of the year: Venus

The Moon in Virgo begins the rulership of time even if it's a day birth. The Sun is in the 8th place and the Moon is in the place of her joy (the 3rd), therefore the Moon is the initiator.

The Moon rules the time for 2 years, since she is in Virgo which is 2 signs away from Cancer.

PERIOD	RULER	YEARS
1980	MOON	2
1982	MERCURY	8
1990	VENUS	5
1995	SUN	6
2001	MARS	5
2006	JUPITER	9
2015	SATURN	7
2022	MOON	2

Following the Moon is Mercury who gets 8 years, because he is in Aquarius which is 8 signs away from his diurnal domicile Gemini.

Next in the ascending order is Venus. She is in Pisces which is 5 signs away from her diurnal domicile Libra, thus Venus gets 5 years.

Following Venus is the Sun, who is in Aquarius, which is 6 signs away from Leo, thus he gets 6 years of rulership.

Mars gets 5 years, because he is in Virgo which is 5 signs away from his diurnal domicile Aries.

Jupiter is in Virgo, 9 signs away from his diurnal domicile of Sagittarius, thus getting 9 years.

Lastly, the furthest away and slowest Saturn who is in Virgo, 7 signs away from his diurnal domicile Aquarius gets 7 years.

The native got married on the 12th of October **in the year 2019, thus in the period ruled by Saturn,** who rules the 7th place. He is placed in the 3rd place of marriage ceremonies and he rules the Lot of Marriage (14 degrees of Capricorn).

EXAMPLE 2
(from chapter 5, example 2)

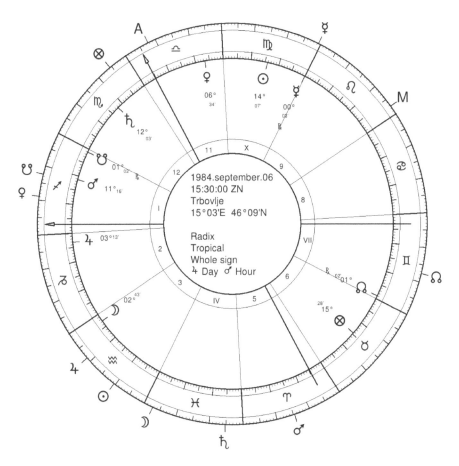

Event: Wedding
Date: 29th of May, 2019
Age: 34
Cycle ruler: Venus
Profection: Libra / 11th place
Ruler of the year: Venus

The Sun is the sect light. He is in the 10th place, therefore the Sun is the initiator. He gets 1 year, because he is in Virgo, the 2nd sign from Leo.

Mars is in Sagittarius, which is 8 signs away from his diurnal domicile Aries, thus he get 8 years.

Jupiter is in Capricorn, which is one sign away from his diurnal domicile Sagittarius, thus he gets 1 year.

Saturn gets 9 years, because he is in Scorpio, which is 9 signs away from his diurnal domicile Aquarius.

The Moon is in Aquarius, which is 7 signs away from Cancer, therefore she gets 7 years.

Venus is in her own diurnal domicile Libra, getting 12 years and her period is still running in the time of writing this book.

PERIOD	RULER	YEARS
1984	SUN	1
1985	MARS	8
1993	JUPITER	1
1994	SATURN	9
2003	MOON	7
2010	MERCURY	3
2013	VENUS	12
2025	SUN	1

The native got married on the 29th of May **in the year 2019, thus in the period ruled by Venus,** who is in the 11th place in her domicile.

EXAMPLE 3
(From chapter 6, examples 3 & 4)

Here I will list two events of childbirth which we saw in chapter 6. This example is interesting, because the two births took place under different time-lords by Trails of the Stars.

Event 1: Birth of daughter (1st child)
Date: 2th of February, 2013
Age: 33
Cycle ruler: Venus
Profection: Sagittarius / 10th place
Ruler of the year: Jupiter

Event 2: Birth of son (2nd child)
Date: 27th of October, 2016 (at 16:01)
Age: 36
Cycle ruler: Sun
Profection: Pisces / 1st place
Ruler of the year: Jupiter

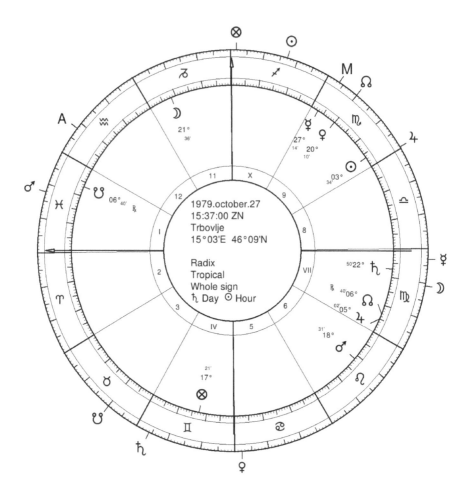

The Moon is the initiator, because the Sun is in the cadent 9th place and she is above the horizon in the 11th place. She is in Capricorn, which is 6 signs away from Cancer, thus she rules for 6 years.

Mercury is in Scorpio, which is 5 signs away from his diurnal domicile Gemini, therefore he gets 5 years.

Venus is also in Scorpio, only 1 sign away from her diurnal domicile Libra, thus ruling for only 1 year.

The Sun is in Scorpio, 3 signs away from Leo, therefore the Sun rules for 3 years.

Mars is in Leo, 4 signs away from his diurnal domicile Aries, getting 4 years.

Jupiter in Virgo is 9 signs away from his diurnal domicile Sagittarius, thus he gets 9 years.

Saturn is also in Virgo, 7 signs away from his diurnal domicile Aquarius, getting 7 years.

PERIOD	RULER	YEARS
1979	MOON	6
1985	MERCURY	5
1990	VENUS	1
1991	SUN	3
1994	MARS	4
1998	JUPITER	9
2007	SATURN	7
2014	MOON	6
2020	MERCURY	5

The first child was born in the period of Saturn while the second child was born in the period of the Moon. Saturn rules the 11th place while the Moon rules the 5th place and is situated in the 11th. Additionally, Saturn is the ruler of the Lot of Children 2.

EXAMPLE 4

(from chapter 7, example 5)

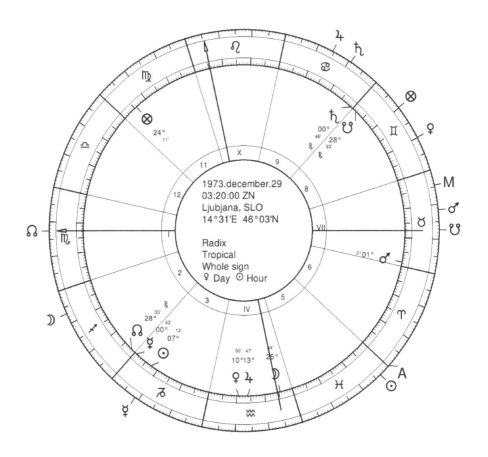

Event: Motorcycle accident and hospitalization

Date: 15th of August, 2016

Age: 43

Cycle ruler: Sun

Profection: Capricorn / 3rd place

Ruler of the year: Saturn

Since the horoscope is nocturnal and the Moon is at the IC in the 4th place she is naturally the initiator. She is in Aquarius, 7 signs away from Cancer, therefore she rules for 7 years.

PERIOD	RULER	YEARS
1973	MOON	7
1980	MERCURY	4
1984	VENUS	9
1993	SUN	5
1998	MARS	6
2004	JUPITER	11
2015	SATURN	6
2021	MOON	5
2026	MERCURY	4

Mercury in Capricorn is 4 signs away from his nocturnal domicile Virgo, getting 4 years.

Venus in Aquarius is 9 signs away from her nocturnal domicile Taurus, therefore she gets 9 years.

The Sun is in Capricorn, 5 signs away from Leo, thus he rules for 5 years.

Mars in Taurus is 6 signs away from his nocturnal domicile Scorpio, getting 6 years.

Jupiter in Aquarius is 11 signs away from his nocturnal domicile Pisces, therefore ruling for 11 years.

Lastly, Saturn who is in Cancer is 6 signs away from his nocturnal domicile Capricorn, thus his rulership extends over a period of 6 years.

The calamity happened in 2016, **in the period ruled by the out-of sect, difficult Saturn, who rules the Lot of Calamity.**

EXAMPLE 5
(from chapter 8, example 3)

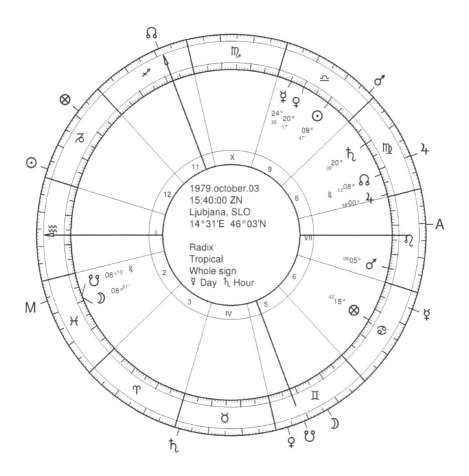

Event: Life-changing travel
Date: Mid January, 2002
Age: 22
Cycle ruler: Venus
Profection: Sagittarius / 11th place
Ruler of the year: Jupiter

179

In this horoscope the Sun is in the 9th place and the Moon is in the 2nd place, below the horizon, therefore the Sun is the initiator. He rules for 2 years, because he is in Libra, two signs away from his domicile Leo.

Next is Mars in Leo, who is 4 signs away from his diurnal domicile Aries, therefore he rules for 4 years.

Jupiter in Virgo rules for 9 years, because he is 9 signs away from his diurnal domicile Sagittarius.

Saturn in Virgo is 7 signs away from his diurnal domicile Aquarius, therefore he rules for 7 years.

The Moon is Pisces, which is 8 signs away from Cancer, giving her 8 years of rulership.

PERIOD	RULER	YEARS
1979	SUN	2
1981	MARS	4
1985	JUPITER	9
1994	SATURN	7
2001	MOON	8

The life-changing journey to a far away land happened in the period of the Moon, who is right on the nodal axis, conjunct the South Node and her ruler Jupiter is in the 8th place. As we saw in the delineation of her horoscope and Solar return, the 8th house was very much involved in this turning point in her life, as were Jupiter and the Moon.

COMMENTS

As we can see, the use of an additional time-lord system can be a valuable tool which enables us to identify a context for profections and Solar returns. In astrological forecasting confluence has to be present. When a theme is confirmed through at least three different timing methods, there is a greater chance that what is indicated will actually manifest.

The Trails of the Stars time-lord technique has proven to be quite effective and I believe that its further development might be beneficial. Simultaneous time-lords from both luminaries (not just the initiator) might reveal more about manifestations from our own volition (the Sun) and what manifests in our lives in a more passive / receptive manner (the Moon).

APPENDIX 1
EXAMPLE HOROSCOPES DATA

CHAPTER 5 (Relationships & marriages)

EXAMPLE 1:
July 16th, 1976, 07:57, Seattle, 122°19′W, 47°36′N, United States

EXAMPLE 2:
September 6th, 1984, 15:30, Trbovlje, 15°03′E, 46°09′N, Slovenia

EXAMPLE 3:
November 2nd, 1960, 04:30, Trbovlje, 15°03′E, 46°09′N, Slovenia

EXAMPLE 4:
February 4th, 1980, 15:01, Zottegem, 03°48′E, 50°52′N, Belgium

EXAMPLE 5:
August 14th, 1979, 18: 16, Trbovlje, 15°03′E, 46°09′N, Slovenia

CHAPTER 6 (Childbirth)

EXAMPLE 1:
November 9th, 1978, 12:11, Slovenj Gradec, 15°04′E, 46°30′N, Slovenia

EXAMPLE 2:
July 25th, 1953, 16:15, Krmelj, 15°11′E, 45°48′N, Slovenia

EXAMPLES 3 & 4:
October 27th, 1979, 15:37, Trbovlje, 15°03′E, 46°09′N, Slovenia

EXAMPLE 5:
October 17th, 1972, 12:40, Kranj, 14°21′E, 46°14′N, Slovenia

CHAPTER 7 (Illnesses, accidents & surgeries)

EXAMPLE 1:
August 14th, 1979, 18: 16, Trbovlje, 15°03'E, 46°09'N, Slovenia

EXAMPLES 2 & 3:
July 25th, 1953, 16:15, Krmelj, 15°11'E, 45°48'N, Slovenia

EXAMPLE 4:
July 6th, 1973, 20:00, Ljubljana, 14°31'E, 46°03'N, Slovenia

EXAMPLE 5:
December 29th, 1973, 03:20, Ljubljana, 14°31'E, 46°03'N, Slovenia

CHAPTER 8 (Milestones & turning points)

EXAMPLE 1:
December 20th, 1988, 16:30, Chennai, 80°16'E, 13°05'N, India

EXAMPLE 2:
October 16th, 1979, 06:55, Ljubljana, 14°31'E, 46°03'N, Slovenia

EXAMPLE 3:
October 3rd, 1979, 15:40, Ljubljana, 14°31'E, 46°03'N, Slovenia

EXAMPLE 4:
August 26th, 1972, 12:46, Kranj, 14°21'E, 46°14'N, Slovenia

EXAMPLE 5:
February 17th, 1961, 01:10, Steyr, 14°25'E, 48°02'N, Austria

APPENDIX 2
NOTES & BIBLIOGRAPHY

1. Time-lord systems are different ways to determine which planet is ruling a particular period in the native's life. The planet that rules the period is called time-lord or *chronokratōr* in classical Greek.

2. Primary directions are a timing method where on planet or point is carried towards another in primary motion (diurnal rotation) and were a popular timing method in classical astrology.

3. Vettius Valens, *Anthology*, book 3, chapter 5

4. Claudius Ptolemy, *Tetrabiblos*, book 1, chapter 7

5. Muhammad Imran, source: internet: https://astroimran.com/wp-content/uploads/2017/12/3-Bhrigu-Chakra-with-Cycle-Ruler.pdf

6. Claudius Ptolemy, *Tetrabiblos*, book 4, chapter 10

7. Dorotheus of Sidon, *Carmen Astrologicum*, book 2, chapter 2

8. Vettius Valens, *Anthology*, book 2, (to find the marriage lot), (same reference for the Lot of Husband)

9. Dorotheus, *Carmen Astrologicum*, book 2, chapter 5,

10. Julius Firmicus Maternus, *Mathesis*, book 6, chapter 32

11. Rhetorius, *Compendium*, chapter 1

12. Dorotheus of Sidon, *Carmen Astrologicum*, book 2, chapter 10

13. Vettius Valens, *Anthology*, book 2, chapter 39 – same reference for both, the Lot of Daughters and the Lot of Sons

14. Vettius Valens, *Anthology*, book 4, chapter 16

15. Rhetorius, *Compendium*, chapter 43

16. Porphyry, *Introduction*, 21; the planet that is earlier in the zodiacal order is said to overcome the planet that is later in the zodiacal order, either through a square or a trine aspect. Such an aspect is thought to be superior (superior trine or superior square).

17. Dorotheus of Sidon, *Carmen Astrologicum*, book 4, 1-45

18. Vettius Valens, *Anthology*, book 4, chapter 17

19. Aswin Subramanyan, *Firdaria – Periods of life*, 2021

20. Jaimini's Upadesha Sutra – an ancient astrological text of India, supposedly written by sage Jaimini who established the Purva-mimamsa school of Vedic thought.

ABOUT ME

I was born and raised in central Slovenia and my quest into the mystery of life began early in my childhood. During my life I experienced many injuries to the body and other health problems which made me hungry for an understanding of why there is suffering and how this manifested world operates. When the 8th place of my horoscope became highlighted I got into mysticism, explored mythologies of different cultures and my quest eventually led me to India where I traveled far and wide, from the south all the way to the Himalayas, gathering precious experiences and knowledge. Soon I got actively involved with a particular branch of Vedic spirituality which led me to the study of Bhagavad-Gita, Sri Isopanishad and Bhagavata Purana along with other works of Indian spiritual literature. Since philosophy and astrology are deeply connected I was soon intrigued by it. Being readily available, I began to study tropical modern Western astrology. I studied on my own, with the help of various books, read horoscopes for my friends, examined various charts and was generally quite happy with the development of my practice, but I was still intrigued by the Indian astrological techniques and concepts, since my philosophical background was Vedic. But, I had difficulty switching over due to the difference in zodiac being used. I was set on the tropical zodiac and I was ready to switch to Indian Vedic astrology only if I would find convincing arguments in favor of the sidereal zodiac. To my great surprise I came across Vedic astrologers who were using the tropical zodiac. I was delighted to see that Indian astrology is not necessarily bound to sidereal zodiac. After some exploration of Indian astrological systems, I felt at home in Jaimini's system of astrology which attracted me by its mystique, elegance, simplicity and profoundness. My interest in ancient astrology eventually brought me back to the West and I began studying what is today known as Hellenistic astrology. I was amazed by its orderly, very rational and systematic approach and also by its incredible similarity to Indian astrology. Today this forms the basis of my work, but I also incorporate certain elements of Indian astrology. I find that the two systems complement each other beautifully and if there is something I enjoy very much it is synthesis.

Since I strongly believe in balance I also enjoy art, specifically music which compliments my rational endeavors in astrology beautifully. I'm a passionate music producer, world flutist, percussionist and synthesist. I've also been practicing Rei-ki healing for many years for which I am extremely grateful as it has been a valuable gift and a great aid on my path. I enjoy nature, especially mountains, which are my biggest inspiration and I love to sit in silence and simply observe Life.

A form of Life,
Rok Koritnik

Made in United States
Troutdale, OR
12/12/2023

15569084R00119